Living Together,
Married or Single:
Your Legal
Rights

NORA LAVORI

Living Together, Married or Single: Your Legal Rights

PERENNIAL LIBRARY
Harper & Row, Publishers
New York, Hagerstown, San Francisco, London

Designed by Eve Kirch Callahan

First edition: PERENNIAL LIBRARY, 1976

LIBRARY OF CONGRESS CATALOG CARD NUMBER: 76–20395

STANDARD BOOK NUMBER: 06–080382–7

76 77 78 79 80 5 4 3 2 1

To my family,
by blood and by marriage.

Contents

Preface

The law is a wealth of questions repeatedly asked and answered. It is a dynamic process rather than a set of rigid rules. Certain principles endure. But the way they are applied changes as reality and as our understanding of reality evolve. The law concerning family relationships is in a particular state of flux. This flux reflects the fact that great changes are occurring in the nature of these relationships.

This book is my rendering of the state of the law concerning living together as of July 1976. But it is not a substitute for legal counsel. If you have questions of a legal nature, you would be wise to consult a qualified person who can tailor a response to your individual needs at that moment.

Many people have helped with this book, both in its inspiration and in its expression. I would like to give special thanks to Eleanor Jackson Piel, Esq., and Gerard Piel, who have been true mentors to me; and to Marjory D. Fields, Esq., for her comments and suggestions on the manuscript.

I would also like to thank Rhonda Copelon, Esq., Veronika Kraft, Esq., and Elizabeth M. Schneider, Esq., for reviewing parts of the manuscript; and Cathy Giammarino, who carefully typed it. Finally, I would like to thank David B. Sterling for his encouragement and enlightenment.

1 / Living Together and the Law

The Cast

Veronica and Rob: artists, in their thirties. They have lived together for six years and have no intention of ever marrying. They do not want children. They believe that marriage is a sexist institution and that it would harm rather than help their relationship. Both are beginning to be recognized in the art world. They live by their art work and occasional jobs. Rob owns a Rauschenberg and a Lichtenstein. Otherwise they have no property of value except bank accounts in their own names.

Anne and Jon: in their mid-twenties. They met in college and have been living together for five years. Both believe that a marriage license means nothing without a good relationship, and they want to avoid falling into the sex roles that are characteristic of so many marriages. Anne's parents are greatly distressed by her living situation. This has put a strain on their relationship. But both feel that they should not marry just to please her parents. This year, Anne and Jon have begun to feel that they know each other well enough to make a legal commitment. They have set a wedding date.

Carl and Karen: in their early forties. Both have

recently left the Catholic clergy. Their lives have changed radically. They want to marry and bring a child into the world, but they do not want to make such a commitment too suddenly. They decide to live together.

Judith and Martin: in their early fifties. Martin is divorced and Judith is in the process of getting a divorce. They do not wish to rush into marriage again, although they both believe in it. They are living together while they get to know each other better and Judith's divorce comes through.

Eric and Sara: in their mid-twenties. They lived together for two years—long enough to discover that they didn't wish to continue to do so. They split up amicably; each took what he or she had contributed.

Angela and Michael: in their mid-thirties. They have lived together for eight years. Their child is now two years old. They are both feminists and say they have a conscientious objection to marriage.

Elizabeth and George: in their early seventies. They are widow and widower and have retired. They live together for companionship and sex. They are past the point of caring what other people think—and their social security is higher than it would be if they married.

These are among the characters in this book. They share a life-style. For one reason or another, temporarily or permanently, they all reject marriage. What legal problems might they encounter? How will the law treat them? How would the law treat them if they were married?

How Many People Live Together without Being Married to Each Other?

Living together is a difficult phenomenon to measure. First of all, what is it? sleeping over? full-time residence at his/her place but paying rent on another to keep up appearances? or each of you calling the same place your official home?[1] Secondly, if someone asked you if you were living together, how many of you would (*a*) be brave enough to answer truthfully or (*b*) feel that it was nobody else's business? Until living together becomes a little more acceptable, giving the truth is a problem. And thirdly, few people have yet cared to ask how many people are living together.

Despite the obstacles to obtaining information, living together appears to be increasingly popular—not only among students, but also among members of the larger community.

The U.S. Census Bureau figures for 1960 reveal that 34,640 men and women were reported as living together. In 1970, there were 285,696. In those census years, people were not asked, "Are you living together?" but in some way they indicated that they were. It takes a certain kind of person to answer a question that is not asked—especially where the truthful answer is not socially acceptable. Therefore, these figures may be low. In view of the changing configuration of the "family," the Census Bureau expects to make an effort to obtain figures on "partnering" in the 1980 census. Assuming the relative validity of these figures, however, there was an eightfold increase in the number of men and women living together from 1960 to 1970. While it is difficult to make a reliable prediction based on the figures, the Bureau guesstimates that some half million men and women were living together in 1976.[2]

On the more subjective side, divorce lawyers and marriage counselors find that men and women who are living together appear increasingly among their clientele. Beyond this, take stock of your friends and acquaintances. It is probably not too presumptuous to say that most people know or know of couples who are living together without being married to each other.

Why Do People Live Together?

The reasons for living together are many and varied. Sometimes the reasons expressed may not be the real reasons at work: we are in the midst of re-evaluating our social institutions, and we may not be capable of understanding the forces motivating our behavior. Be that as it may, these are some of the reasons given:

1. A desire to avoid the sex-stereotyped allocation of roles associated with marriage. Things like he is the breadwinner, she is the chief cook and bottle washer. He is cool, calm, collected, and rational; she is hysterical, harried, and emotional. The husband and wife made famous by television advertising.

2. A belief that marriage is designed to protect children, coupled with a desire not to have children—i.e., a feeling that marriage is unnecessary or irrelevant if no children are involved.

3. A lack of readiness to commit oneself. This

may be a generalized feeling of personally being unprepared to make a commitment or a feeling of being unsure about the specific individual. The people who feel this way want to become more familiar with each other before taking any vows.

4. A philosophical conclusion that you cannot predict what you will feel in the future and that you should not make promises that you don't know you will be able to or will even want to keep. This is 1950's A-bomb thinking: don't count on there being a future.

5. A conscientious objection to marriage—i.e., the belief that the state has no right to be involved with matters so intimate as one's relationship with another.

6. A desire to avoid the expense and involvement of a possible divorce.

7. A belief that legal sanction of a relationship is irrelevant and meaningless—what counts is how the people feel and behave toward each other—also known as the substance-form dichotomy.

People who have lived together and since married say that living together enabled them to become more comfortable with each other and to more objectively evaluate their relationship. Objective evaluation of a marriage may be more difficult because you have a vested interest in its continuance.

Both those who see living together as a trial marriage and those who see it as a permanent life-style agree that the anti-establishment position in which you place yourself by living together has great value. It tends to let you be yourself more. You do not have to act married, because you are not married. If you are a woman, you are less likely to feel guilty about not cleaning house or washing his under-wear. Similarly, if you are a man, you are less likely to feel guilty about not being able to meet all the household expenses by yourself or about not taking out the garbage. These types of behavior may not be expected of you and you need not expect them of yourself. Living together offers the opportunity to develop yourselves and your relationship in a unique and personal way.

There is an additional psychological bonus to living together. It is that you have the privilege of feeling that you are doing exactly what you want to do all the time. That is not to say that there are never moments when you wish you had never laid eyes on your partner. But at those times, you can always say to yourself, "Nobody's forcing me to be here." People like to feel that they are acting vol-untarily. In fact, one function of socialization is to make people think they are doing what they want to do. The problem is that you can't fool your un-conscious. If you feel you are being coerced, your unconscious will register anger.

When married people come in conflict, they may well feel trapped. But they cannot say, "Nobody's forcing me to be here," because someone *is* forcing them to be there—the state. What they are doing is voluntary only in the very abstract sense that they chose to marry—once. People who are living together choose to marry every day. The anger that a married person feels toward the state, or the society that mandates and fosters marriage, may often be directed toward husband or wife. So the spouse can become a jailer and a symbol of all that is coercive in our lives. People who are living to-gether can never get too far with this fiction because they are presumably together voluntarily. If either feels trapped (and does not respond by abandoning the relationship), he or she must inquire into his/her feelings more deeply than is necessary for automatically placing blame on a mate.

The extensive and profound questioning of marriage that we as a society are experiencing is to a great extent a product of the control we have gained over reproduction through contraception and abortion. Like nothing else, contraception and abortion have stimulated the emancipation of women. As the condition of women evolves, so will the nature of marriage.

In a marriage as it has been and is defined by law, the husband is required to support his wife; the wife is required to provide certain services including cooking, cleaning, and child-rearing. If either fails to perform his or her obligations, the other has grounds for divorce on the theory of abandonment. The basis for this division of labor most likely lies in the biological fact that women bear children.

But this division of labor is no longer *necessary*. The biology has not changed. It is still women alone who are capable of bearing children. But through contraception and abortion, women have gained the ability to control reproduction: A woman can choose whether and when she will bear a child. She has more options available to her than when she was at the beck and call of motherhood.

Women have begun to exercise these options more extensively. Statistics show that the traditional division of labor, where the husband works in the paid labor force and the wife works in the home, is no longer typical of marriages in the United States. In 1974, 43 percent of all married women whose husbands were present in the home, 54 percent of all women with children six to seventeen years old, and nearly 37 percent of the mothers with children under six participated in the labor force.[3]

However, although the possibilities and the experiences of women are changing, the legal accoutrements of marriage haven't kept up with the changes. The law of marriage should be redefined to accommodate the changes in our understanding of the roles men and women may take in our society. While the process of adapting the institution to the reality goes on, however, people will continue to seek alternatives to traditional marriage.

Marriage as a legal institution now has the function of giving the relationship between a man and a woman meaning in our society. It defines sexual territory, creates a shorthand way of determining who gets your property when you die, and specifies who is required to support whom. The need for such an institution remains because it helps to order our society. But its form must change because the presumptions on which it is based are largely obsolete. When both husband and wife have the mutual obligation to support each other, when each may obtain alimony based on need, when the tax and social security laws no longer penalize the wife who works outside the home, when the legal attributes of marriage better reflect how we view ourselves, marriage will be a more viable institution. But the nature of marriage is not going to change overnight. And even if it does become more attractive, it will probably never meet everyone's needs.

Our legal system should accept alternatives to marriage. Living together can be an effective way for people to find out if they are well suited for each other. It offers people the chance to see if they possess the adaptability that is required for a satisfying marriage. That is not to say that people who live together before marriage ultimately have satisfying marriages. We do not know whether theirs are more happy or durable than marriages of people who never lived together. But the more knowledge you have of your proposed mate, and of how *you* function within the relationship, the greater are your chances of choosing well. If more knowledge helps people to make better decisions for themselves, the society will be strengthened by the phenomenon of living together.

Living together as a permanent way of life should also be accepted. It is a social fact, for better or for worse, and it will not disappear even if dealt with repressively. The forces leading people to live together rather than to marry will not be eliminated by making it a crime. The existence of such an alternative need not undermine marriage. In fact, it may discourage from getting married those who would merely go through the motions.

People who are living together should for the most part be treated as singles. No penalties should be inflicted on them, nor can they be justified, because of their relationship. Certainly, children born out of wedlock should not be punished because of their parents' marital status. They should be treated as if they were legitimate. The law should give people who live together the means to protect their own interests adequately—for example, through making contracts and wills—and then leave well enough alone.

Putting the Law in Its Place

Knowing the law is only one aspect of bringing reality to bear on your decision to marry or to live together. That decision is by no means entirely rational, nor should it be. The psychological and emotional motives to be considered are equally, if not more, valid. Knowing the law will only help you to feel more comfortable with the situation you choose. It will free you to concentrate on what is truly important—defining better ways for you to build a relationship with a partner.

Throughout this book you will encounter the word "discrimination." It is emotionally charged. But it simply means that in substantially similar situations, people are treated differently for reasons that do not hold up under rational examination. In the legal area of marriage and living together, discrimination based on gender and marital status is rampant. The inequities in the law are being challenged as this book is written. So you must be aware that the law of marriage and living together, like all law, is dynamic, rather than made up of static rules. A statement of what the law is, is just a prediction at a given moment of how a court will decide a specific issue raised in a specific factual context.[4] As attitudes toward sex, the proper roles of men and women, living together, and marriage change, the law will change. Do not be surprised if you find yourself to be a catalyst of this change.[5]

NOTES

1. This is the definition I prefer.

2. Data from unpublished summary table, "Household Head and Unrelated Partner of Opposite Sex Sharing the Same Living Quarters, for the U.S., 1970 and 1960," based on U.S. Bureau of the Census, *1970 Census of Population,* vol. II, pt. 4B, Table 11, "Persons by Family Characteristics"; and *1960 Census of Population,* vol. II, pt. 4B, Table 15, "Persons by Family Characteristics." The table is available from Dr. Paul C. Glick, Senior Demographer, Population Division, Bureau of the Census, U.S. Department of Commerce.

3. U.S. Department of Labor, Employment Standards Administration, Women's Bureau, *1975 Handbook on Women Workers,* Bulletin no. 297 (Washington, D.C., 1976), p. 3.

4. The decisions of all courts are not of equal weight. Generally, the higher the court, the more authoritative the decision. Therefore, it is useful to know which court decided the issue. In the federal system, a case is brought in a district court, appealed to a circuit court and then to the U.S. Supreme Court, if it grants certiorari (agrees to hear the case). In the state-court systems, there is an analogous three-tiered structure. The highest court in a state is usually, but not always, called the Supreme Court.

5. Much of the material in this book is relevant to homosexual, as well as heterosexual, couples. However, in the interest of brevity, legal issues peculiar to homosexual couples are not discussed. They are dealt with in detail in other publications such as *The Rights of Gay People: The Basic ACLU Guide to a Gay Person's Rights* by E. Carrington Boggan, Marilyn G. Haft, Charles Lister, and John P. Rupp (New York: Avon Books, 1975).

2 / Common-Law Marriage and Cohabitation

"It is better to marry than to burn"—so said the medieval clergy. But what they meant by marriage and what we mean by marriage are two different things. During the twelfth century, the church defined marriage as *sponsalia per verba de praesenti*—espousal by words of the present tense: "I receive you as mine." That is what has come to be known as common-law marriage. In those days, common-law marriage was the rule rather than the exception. Although the church tried to persuade the "heathens" that its approval was indispensable, no marriage ceremony was required. People did marry through ritual—Anglo-Saxon, Jewish, Roman, Germanic—but the wide variety of rituals made it difficult for the church to single out one for all. During the twelfth century in England, the homeland of our legal system, the church's word regarding marriage was law. A papal divorce granted around 1143 exemplifies the doctrine of the canon law: "A marriage solemnly celebrated in church, a marriage of which a child had been born was set aside as null in favor of an earlier marriage constituted by a mere exchange of consenting words."[1] In 1215, Pope Innocent III required the publishing of the banns of marriage—that is, an announcement to the community of a proposed marriage with the urging that any who knew of an impediment should come forward. But while "publishing the banns" made marriage easier to prove, it did not abolish marriage by mutual consent.

Ironically, the courts of law began to require more than the church, through the ecclesiastical courts, did. They were often called upon to decide whether a woman or child was entitled to an inheritance. Thus they were drawn into determining whether a marriage was valid and whether a child was legitimate. Essentially, the validity of marriage became a problem of proof. Because of that, in the mid-nineteenth century, England's highest court decided that henceforth the presence of a clergyman was required for a marriage to be valid.

However, our present-day marriage ceremony contains some vestiges of the old ways. Even today, while the presence of a representative of the state or a member of the clergy is required, he/she does not literally marry you but merely acts as a witness— you marry yourselves by words indicating your present intent to take each other as husband and wife.

Nowadays you don't hear it so much, but just a few years ago it wasn't unusual to hear reference to "my common-law husband" or "my common-law wife." Then it was a polite way of talking about people who weren't ceremonially or officially married. The term has come into disuse, most likely because today when people reject marriage they are rejecting all kinds of marriage. Who wants to be a wife or a husband at all! In addition, people are becoming more relaxed about living together, so they can be honest about the relationship and not turn it into something it is not. However, there are still a lot of misconceptions about common-law marriage.

What Is Common-Law Marriage?

Common-law marriage is a legal marriage that has been brought about without an official ceremony. It exists when a man and woman live together and consider themselves husband and wife (unlike most people who are living together today) and communicate this to others by their behavior. For instance, the woman may be known as Mrs. So-and-so; the man may refer to her as "my wife, Isabel." In letters to each other, they may refer to each other as husband and wife. The man may support the woman; she may care for him, the house, and any children they have. Whether a common-law marriage exists is a question of fact to be determined by looking at all the behavior of the people involved. Do they consider themselves married? Do they manifest their intention to be married by their behavior?

That's just what you thought? Right. But what most people do not know is that common-law marriage is recognized in only thirteen states—Alabama, Colorado, Georgia, Idaho, Iowa, Kansas, Montana, Ohio, Oklahoma, Pennsylvania, Rhode Island, South Carolina, Texas—and Washington, D.C. Common-law marriage is disappearing in the United States for the same reason it disappeared in England— the problem of proof. Other states will recognize a common-law marriage if it is entered into in a state where it is permitted. Accordingly, if you lived together in Pennsylvania and satisfied Pennsylvania's requirements for a common-law marriage, then moved to New York, your marriage would be valid in New York. But if you began living together in New York, which does not have common-law marriage, you would not have a common-law marriage even if you told everyone you were married. States that do not have common-law marriage require a marriage ceremony and a license.

How Is Common-Law Marriage Relevant to People Who Are Just Living Together?

If you are living together in a state that recognizes common-law marriage, you face the possibility of having the law decide that you have one. This may arise when you split up or when one of you dies and the other tries to assert the existence of a valid marriage. Of course, if a court finds that you did indeed have a common-law marriage, you have all the privileges and must endure all the obligations of marriage. The only way to avoid having a common-law marriage imposed upon you in states that recognize such marriages is by making sure no one thinks you are married.

Can You Marry by Agreement?

Not exactly. Except in the states that permit common-law marriage, a marriage must be "solemnized." That means there must be a ceremony at which an authorized person such as a minister or a judge presides. The amount of participation required of the person performing the ceremony varies from state to state. In New York, for example, no particular ceremony is prescribed, but you must declare before the magistrate or a member of the clergy and in the presence of one witness that you take each other as husband and wife. Contrary to general opinion, the words "till death do us part," "I do," and the like, are not required by law but are mere tradition.

New York also permits a marriage to be solemnized by a written contract of marriage signed by both parties in the presence of two witnesses and acknowledged before a judge.[2] "Acknowledged" means that all those who sign the contract must identify the signatures as their own.

Is It a Crime for a Man and Woman Who Are Not Married to Each Other to Live Together or to Have Intercourse?

The law varies from state to state. Cohabitation—living together as if husband and wife—is a crime in twenty states. Fornication—sexual intercourse between a man and woman who are unmarried—is a crime in sixteen states and Washington, D.C. (See Table 1, page 33.) If one of you is married and you have intercourse or live together, you are committing adultery, which is a crime in most states as well as grounds for divorce. You may also be vulnerable to a charge of bigamy.

The penalties for the crime of cohabitation range from a warning by the judge in New Mexico to a $1,000 maximum fine in Kansas and a three-year maximum jail sentence in Arizona and Massachusetts. In Alabama, you can be sentenced to six months' hard labor. Note that even though common-law marriage is valid in Kansas, you can be prosecuted for living together!

The penalties for the crime of fornication range from a $10 maximum fine in Rhode Island to a $500 maximum fine and a one-year maximum jail sentence in South Carolina. (See Table 2, page 36.)

For most unmarried couples, these laws are a paper dragon. There is only a slight chance that your neighbor will trot down to the police station and inform on you. Furthermore, these crimes are not among prosecutors' favorites. In a recent New Jersey case, the court noted that a study found that prosecutors favored the repeal of these statutes in a ratio of seven to one. According to the court, the author of the study "concluded that the majority of prosecutors apparently view fornication and cohabitation as crimes which are, in a sense, punishable by marriage."[3]

Nevertheless, cohabitation and fornication are still on the books as crimes, and even though the incidence of prosecution is low, you have reason to be uneasy. You may be unlucky enough to live in a state where the prosecutor is disturbed by nonmarital sex or has nothing better to do. In addition, the fact that intercourse and living together are criminal acts may be relevant to other legal actions in which you are involved. For example, in a recent New Jersey case, a man was charged with rape. He successfully defended against the charge by establishing that the alleged victim consented to intercourse. Although he was acquitted of rape, he was then charged with fornication.[4]

The fact that fornication and cohabitation are crimes has other implications too. June Clark was the mother of two illegitimate children. She applied for welfare benefits. The welfare department asked her to get an order of paternity identifying the father of the children so that she could compel him to support them. In the course of the paternity proceeding, June acknowledged that she was living with Charles Barr, who was the father of the children. Both June and Charles were then prosecuted for fornication. In technical language, June had incriminated herself. Fortunately for June and Charles, the Fifth Amendment provides a privilege against self-incrimination. It says that you do not have to make any statements that might be against your own interest. The court reversed their convictions and dismissed the indictment. It said:

> The approval or disapproval of sexual promiscuity is not involved here. Basically, we are concerned with whether needy children should be deprived of public assistance because their mother will not seek it for fear of prosecution for fornication. This means punishment of the children for the immorality of their mother—a result inconsistent with the high purpose of the public welfare program. . . .[5]

The self-incrimination problem can arise in other contexts as well. You do have the Fifth Amendment on your side. But you should not wait until you have been indicted for fornication to exercise it. You have a right to remain silent about your sexual activity if fornication or cohabitation is a crime in your state.

Are the laws against cohabitation or fornication constitutional? There are four basic legal arguments against them: (1) they violate the equal-protection clause of the Fourteenth Amendment because they are erratically and selectively prosecuted, (2) they violate the due-process clause of the Fourteenth Amendment in that they fail to provide adequate notice of the behavior proscribed, (3) they violate the right to privacy recognized in case law in that they interfere with matters of sexual privacy without a showing of compelling state interest,[6] and (4) they violate the First Amendment right to freedom of expression in that they impose a standard of morality that has its origins in religion and they therefore constitute an establishment of religion.

The equal-protection clause of the Fourteenth Amendment requires a law to be nondiscriminatory on its face and in its application. Laws that are enforced selectively or according to an impermissible rationale such as race or gender, therefore, may violate the equal-protection clause.

The due-process clause of the Fourteenth Amendment requires the wording of a law to be sufficiently clear to inform people of what they are or are not permitted to do. A law that speaks of "lewd and lascivious" conduct, for example, may be unconstitutionally vague.

The First Amendment prohibits laws respecting an establishment of religion or prohibiting the free exercise of religion. A law that mandates particular religious practices or that stands in the way of the exercise of a religious belief might run afoul of the First Amendment.

The U.S. Supreme Court has not yet addressed itself to the constitutionality of these laws. Lower courts have upheld them. Their response to the equal-protection argument is that there has been no showing that the law is applied in a discriminatory way. Their response to the due-process argument is that the laws do provide adequate notice. Their response to the privacy argument is that interference is justified by the state's compelling interest in preventing venereal disease and illegitimacy. Their response to the First Amendment argument is that although the laws originated in religious beliefs, they have enough secular justifications—prevention of V.D. and illegitimacy—to support their constitutionality.[7]

By far the most persuasive argument is that these laws unduly interfere with the individual's right to privacy. A state may interfere with a person's right to privacy only on a showing that the law in question is necessary to accomplish a permissible state policy. Let's assume that the prevention of illegitimacy and V.D. are valid state objectives. Are laws against fornication and cohabitation a *necessary* means to achieve these ends? Perhaps at one time—before contraceptives and abortion—they were. But now they appear to be overbroad. If the legislature wanted to curb illegitimacy, it would be better off encouraging contraception. If it wanted to curb V.D., it would be better off establishing medical and educational programs. The relationship between making intercourse and living together criminal and the prevention of V.D. and illegitimacy is so attenuated that one wonders whether these laws are not mere pretexts for legislating certain moral values.

The laws are irrelevant to the prevention of illegitimacy and V.D. in part because they will not be obeyed. In this respect, the laws against sex are like the laws against marijuana or alcohol. An important premise of our legal system is that it works only by consent of the governed. People must basically agree with a law; if they do not, they will ignore it. If people do not feel that nonmarital sex is an offense against society, they will not be deterred by the law. The authority inherent in the entire system of law is thereby diminished.

Can You Be Denied Naturalization Because You Are Living with Someone?

You can be denied naturalization as a United States citizen for bad moral character. Bad moral character normally means, for example, that you have been convicted of a serious crime, are an alcoholic or drug addict, or have committed adultery.

For a person to be denied naturalization for adultery, the adultery must endanger an ongoing marriage. Therefore, if you are separated, adultery may not appear to be a good index of bad moral character.[8]

Living together has not been considered a sign of bad moral character. Jeanne Marguerite Mortyr, a Swedish national, was living in Oregon with a man to whom she was not married. Her application for naturalization was turned down because of that. The man testified in court that he was willing and able to marry her but she refused. The court decided that she should be naturalized. In his decision, the judge wrote:

> I am convinced that the petitioner has not refused marriage out of whimsey or from a desire to remain uncommitted, but out of a sincere and reasoned belief that marriage in the U.S. is all too often a transient status. She has, in a manner of speaking, formed a conscientious objection to the conventional marriage ceremony. This conviction had led her to

a belief that to celebrate a socially accepted marriage would, for her, be hypocrisy. She believes that it would be intellectually dishonest to enter into lawful wedlock merely to satisfy the Immigration and Naturalization Service.[9]

If you can show a similar conscientious objection to marriage and are in other respects a "fine, upstanding" person, you will probably be able to convince a judge to permit your naturalization. This position has support in other case law. A five-year period of cohabitation before marriage has not barred naturalization,[10] nor has fornication,[11] nor has the fact that a widower fathered a child with an unmarried woman.[12] In fact, in the last case the American child may sponsor its father for purposes of citizenship.

Even if you live in a state that makes fornication or cohabitation a crime, absent conviction, living together does not necessarily show bad moral character for purposes of naturalization. Naturalization is a federal determination and federal standards govern. If there is a conviction, there is a remote possibility that the crime will be considered serious enough to justify denial of naturalization.

TABLE 1

CRIMINAL LAWS AGAINST COHABITATION AND FORNICATION

(Reflects the State of the Law as of 1976)

State	Is Cohabitation a Crime?	Is Fornication a Crime?
Alabama	Yes (14 § 16)	No*
Alaska	Yes (11.40.040)	No*
Arizona	Yes (13 § 222)	No
Arkansas	Yes (41 § 805)	No
California	No	No
Colorado	No	No
Connecticut	No	No
Delaware	No	No
Florida	Yes (798.02)	Yes (798.03)
Georgia	No	Yes (26–2010)
Hawaii	No	Yes (768–17)
Idaho	Yes (18–6603)	Yes (18–6604)
Illinois	Yes (38–11–8)	Yes (38–11–8)
Indiana	Yes (10–4207)	Yes (10–4207)

TABLE 1—*Continued*

State	Is Cohabitation a Crime?	Is Fornication a Crime?
Iowa	No	No
Kansas	Yes (23 § 118)	No
Kentucky	No	No
Louisiana	No	No
Maine	No	No
Maryland	No	No
Massachusetts	Yes (272 § 16)	Yes (272 § 18)
Michigan	Yes (750.335)	No*
Minnesota	No	No
Mississippi	Yes (97–29–1)	Yes (97–29–1)
Missouri	No	No
Montana	No	No
Nebraska	Yes (28–928)	No
Nevada	No	No
New Jersey	No	Yes (2A:110–1)
New Hampshire	No	No
New Mexico	Yes (40–A–10–2)	No
New York	No	No

North Carolina	Yes (14–184)	Yes (14–184)
North Dakota	No	No
Ohio	No	No
Oklahoma	No	No
Oregon	No	No
Pennsylvania	No	No
Rhode Island	No	Yes (11'–6–3)
South Carolina	Yes (16–406)	Yes (16–408)
South Dakota	No	No
Tennessee	No	No
Texas	No	No
Utah	No	Yes (76–7–104)
Vermont	No	No
Virginia	Yes (18.2–345)	Yes (18.2–344)
Washington	No	No
West Virginia	Yes (61–8–4)	Yes (61–8–3)
Wisconsin	Yes (944.20)	Yes (944.15)
Wyoming	Yes (6–86)	No
Puerto Rico	No	No
Washington, D.C.	No	Yes (22–1002)

* The law in this state is ambiguous. In some circumstances, mere acts of sexual intercourse may be considered to violate the statute prohibiting cohabitation.

TABLE 2

PENALTIES FOR THE CRIMES OF COHABITATION AND FORNICATION

State	Cohabitation	Fornication
Alabama	First conviction: min. $100 fine and/or sentence to prison or hard labor for max. 6 mos. Second: min. $300 fine and/or sentence to prison or hard labor for 1 yr. Third: 2 yrs. sentence.	....
Alaska	Max. $500 fine and/or 1–2 yrs. sentence.	....
Arizona	Felony. Max. 3 yrs. sentence.	....
Arkansas	Misdemeanor. First conviction: $20–$100 fine. Second: $100 and max. 1 yr. sentence. Third: 1–3 yrs. sentence.	....
Florida	Misdemeanor. Max. 60 days sentence.	Misdemeanor. Max. 60 days sentence.
Georgia	....	Misdemeanor.
Hawaii	....	$15–50 fine and/or 1–3 mos. sentence.

Idaho	Misdemeanor. Max. $300 fine and/or max. 6 mos. sentence.	Max. $300 fine and/or max. 6 mos. sentence.
Illinois	Misdemeanor. Less than 1 yr. sentence.	Misdemeanor. Less than 1 yr. sentence.
Indiana	Max. $500 fine and/or max. 6 mos. sentence.	Max. $500 fine and/or max. 6 mos. sentence.
Kansas	Misdemeanor. $500–$1000 fine and/or 1–3 mos. sentence.	……
Massachusetts	Max. $300 fine or max. 3 yrs. sentence.	Max. $30 fine or max. 3 mos. sentence.
Michigan	Misdemeanor. Max. $500 fine or max. 1 yr. sentence.	……
Mississippi	Max. $500 fine and 6 mos. sentence.	Max. $500 fine and 6 mos. sentence.
Nebraska	Max. $100 fine and 6 mos. sentence.	Misdemeanor. Max. $50 fine and/or 6 mos. sentence.
New Jersey	……	……
New Mexico	Warning by judge.	……
North Carolina	Misdemeanor. Max. $500 fine and/or 6 mos. sentence.	Misdemeanor. Max. $500 fine and/or 6 mos. sentence.
Rhode Island	……	Max. $10 fine.

TABLE 2—*Continued*

State	Cohabitation	Fornication
South Carolina	$100–$500 fine and/or 6 mos.–1 yr. sentence.	$100–$500 fine and/or 6 mos.–1 yr. sentence.
Utah	....	Max. $299 fine or 6 mos. sentence.
Virginia	Misdemeanor. First conviction: $500 max. fine. Thereafter: $1,000 max. fine and/or 1 yr. sentence.	Misdemeanor. Max. $100 fine.
West Virginia	Misdemeanor. Min. $50 fine and/or min. 6 mos. sentence.	Misdemeanor. Min. $20 fine.
Wisconsin	Max. $500 fine and/or max. 1 yr. sentence.	Max. $200 fine and/or 6 mos. sentence.
Wyoming	Max. $100 fine and/or max. 3 mos. sentence.	....
Washington, D.C.	....	Max. $300 fine and/or 6 mos. sentence.

NOTES

1. Frederick Pollock and Frederick William Maitland, *History of English Law,* vol. II (Cambridge: Cambridge University Press, 1968), p. 367.

2. N.Y.S. Domestic Relations Law, § 11(4) (McKinney's 1964).

3. *State* v. *Saunders,* 130 N.J. Super. 234, 326 A.2d 84, 87 (1974).

4. *Ibid.*

5. *State* v. *Clark,* 58 N.J. 72, 275 A.2d 137, 148 (1971).

6. *Eisenstadt* v. *Baird,* 405 U.S. 438 (1972); and *Griswold* v. *Connecticut,* 381 U.S. 479 (1965).

7. *State* v. *Saunders,* n.3.

8. *In re Schroers,* 336 F. Supp. 1348 (S.D.N.Y. 1971).

9. *In re Mortyr,* 320 F. Supp. 1222 (D.C. Ore. 1970).

10. *Posusta* v. *United States,* 285 F.2d 533 (2nd Cir. 1961).

11. *In re Van Dessel,* 243 F. Supp. 328 (E.D. Pa. 1965).

12. *In re Gartska,* 295 F. Supp. 833 (W.D. Mich. 1969).

3 / Contraception and Abortion

The availability of contraceptives and abortion makes it possible for people to live together without the risk of pregnancy. Sexual relations no longer mean automatic parenthood. So the stability and permanence of the relationship between a man and a woman becomes less important than they are in a society where intercourse and childbearing are virtually synonymous. Where childbearing is consciously chosen and deliberate, the alliance between a man and a woman does not have to be ironclad from the start. It can be more loosely defined, more tentative.

It was not so long ago that contraception and abortion were illegal. Legalization was not easily won. To this day, there are strong efforts to limit the availability of abortion. That is not surprising, since contraception and abortion have a profound effect on the condition of women and on the nature of the family. The implications of our technology are widely feared.

Can You Be Denied Contraception or Abortion Because You Are Unmarried?

No. In 1965, the U.S. Supreme Court decided in *Griswold* v. *Connecticut* that it is unconstitutional for a state law to prohibit the use of contraceptives by married people.[1] In 1972, in *Eisenstadt* v. *Baird,* the Court held that it was unconstitutional for a state law to prohibit their sale to unmarried people.[2]

Nor can you be denied an abortion because you are unmarried. In 1973, "Jane Roe," a pregnant single woman, challenged the Texas statute that made it a crime to procure an abortion except on medical advice, to save the life or health of the mother. The Supreme Court decided that the statute violated her right to personal privacy. The Court didn't address the issue of her marital status directly but relied on the *Baird* decision for the proposition that the right of personal privacy is an individual right not dependent on marital status.[3]

But although you cannot be denied an abortion simply because you are single, you should be aware that you can be denied one on other grounds. Contrary to popular belief, the 1973 abortion decision did not establish that a woman has an *absolute* right to control her own body. The Court said that her right to personal privacy regarding abortion was limited by certain important governmental interests—namely, the interests in maternal health, in maintaining medical standards, and in protecting potential life. That is why you may be required by state law to have your abortion within a certain period of time after conception or under specified hospital conditions.

Can You Be Denied Contraception or Abortion Because You Are a Minor?

The question concerning contraception is unresolved in most states. Until recently a New York statute prohibited the sale or distribution of nonprescription contraceptives (e.g., foams and condoms) to persons under sixteen years of age. Thus a woman under sixteen could obtain a prescription for contraceptives from her doctor but she could not purchase any in a drugstore. The federal district court finally decided that that violated the Fourteenth Amendment.[4]

Similarly, the attorney general of California has decided that a minor female living with her parents does not need their permission to obtain contraceptives.[5] New York and California are probably the most liberal states and it is likely that minors will encounter great difficulty elsewhere in getting contraceptives without parental consent.

As for abortion, the 1973 decisions raised but did not decide the issue of whether a state can require an unmarried minor to obtain parental consent in order to have an abortion.[6] Several states enacted such legislation. But in July 1976, the Supreme Court decided that the Missouri parental-consent statute violated the young woman's right to privacy and was invalid. The Court said, "Constitutional rights do not mature and come into being magically only when one attains the state-defined age of majority. Minors, as well as adults, are protected by the Constitution and possess constitutional rights."[7]

This decision does not mean that *all* parental consent requirements are invalid. It prohibits statutes that give a parent unilateral veto power. However, a statute that *prefers* parental consent but gives a young woman the opportunity to apply to a court for an order allowing abortion without parental consultation may be constitutional.[8]

Can the Person with Whom You Are Living Require You or Forbid You to Have an Abortion? Can He if You Are Married?

After the 1973 abortion decisions, several states enacted laws imposing consent restrictions on a woman's right to abortion. Some said the "father of the fetus" had to consent, others said the "husband" of the pregnant woman had to consent, and still others said that the "husband of a minor wife" had to consent.[9]

The 1973 decisions established that a woman has the absolute right to terminate her pregnancy in the first trimester. After that, her right becomes qualified by the state's interest in maternal and infant health. In July 1976, the Supreme Court held unconstitutional the Missouri statute requiring the husband's written consent to abortion within the first trimester. Since the state itself is prohibited from exercising a veto power during that period, it cannot delegate such a power to the husband. The Court acknowledged the concern a husband has in his wife's pregnancy and in the growth and development of the fetus. But it concluded, "Since it is the woman who physically bears the child and who is the more directly and immediately affected by the pregnancy, as between the two, the balance weighs in her favor."[10]

Although the Court did not speak to the validity of "father of the fetus" statutes, analagous reasoning should apply. The best estimate is that an unwed father cannot compel the mother to have or not have an abortion. The Florida Court of Appeals has held that the alleged father has no right to prevent an unmarried pregnant woman from having an abortion even though he was willing to marry her and to support the child, because according him such a right would be an invasion of her privacy.[11] This attitude toward the unwed father has been bolstered by another case in which the court said that the alleged father did not have to be joined as a party in a woman's suit to compel a hospital to give her an abortion.[12] The case invalidating the Utah law was also based on invasion of privacy.[13]

NOTES

1. *Griswold* v. *Connecticut*, 381 U.S. 479 (1965).

2. *Eisenstadt* v. *Baird*, 405 U.S. 438 (1972).

3. *Roe* v. *Wade*, 410 U.S. 113 (1973).

4. *Population Services International* v. *Wilson*, 383 F. Supp. 543 (S.D.N.Y. 1975).

5. Opinion of November 26, 1974, 1 Family Law Reporter 2068.

6. *Roe* v. *Wade*, n. 3, and *Doe* v. *Bolton*, 410 U.S. 179 (1973).

7. *Planned Parenthood of Central Missouri* v. *Danforth*, 44 United States Law Week 5197, at p. 5204, Docket Nos. 74–1151 and 74–1419.

8. *Bellotti* v. *Baird*, 44 United States Law Week 5221, Docket Nos. 75–73 and 75–109.

9. Father of fetus: Utah, Nebraska. Husband: Arkansas, Colorado, Delaware, Florida, Missouri, New Mexico, Oregon, South Carolina, Washington. Husband of a minor wife: Louisiana, South Dakota.

10. *Planned Parenthood of Central Missouri* v. *Danforth*, p. 5203, n. 6.

11. *Jones* v. *Smith,* Fla. App., 278 So. 2d 339 (1973).
12. *Doe* v. *Bellin Memorial Hospital,* 479 F.2d 756 (7th Cir. 1973).
13. *Doe* v. *Rampton,* 366 F. Supp. 189 (Utah 1973).

4 / Children

Given the availability of contraception and abortion, the kind of children we will discuss in this chapter are not accidents. We are concerned here with the *wanted* illegitimate child—the child brought into the world by a man and a woman who are not married and want to keep it that way. The important question is what are the legal consequences to the child of his or her illegitimacy.

In the days of the Puritans, as written about by Nathaniel Hawthorne, a woman who bore an illegitimate child had to wear a scarlet *A* for adultery as a symbol of her disgrace. Today, the degree of criticism to which an unmarried mother is subject varies with her economic class, ethnic background, age, and other factors. It is likely, however, that the greatest burden the parents of an illegitimate child will bear is not public outrage but having to assure the child all the benefits the law offers to legitimate children.

Attitudes have changed somewhat since that day, and the law is beginning to reflect greater tolerance of illegitimacy. But there are still judges and legislators who see nothing wrong in visiting the "sins" of the parent upon the child or who think that punishing the illegitimate child is the way to reduce illegitimacy.

The biggest issue today in the law of illegitimacy is the relationship between father and child. Should an illegitimate child be entitled to benefits that derive from his/her father? Should the father of an illegitimate child have rights regarding his child? The law is moving toward parity between illegitimate and legitimate children, but it is not there yet. An illegitimate child cannot yet inherit in intestacy (when a person dies without a will) from his/her father unless the father legitimates the child according·to the statute of the state in which he lives. Proof of paternity is not enough. This means that it is easy for an illegitimate child to lose out on an inheritance that is rightfully his/hers.

But until the law views illegitimate and legitimate children as equals, you as the parents will have to be vigilant. Problems arise when you are no longer speaking to each other; therefore, as with all aspects of the law relating to living together, you must prepare in advance for disharmony. In this situation, however, it is not just your future at stake, but that of a dependent human being who did not choose to be born illegitimate.

You must keep in mind as you consider having a child that although you may have few conflicts now, children will bring them out. It has been noted that childless marriages that survive are happier than marriages with children.[1] Children introduce stressful responsibilities that are hard enough to cope with, with society's approval, much less its opprobrium.

Again, the legal dimension in deciding to have children is a small one, but it should loom larger if your child will be illegitimate.

A Word about Terminology

A child born to parents who are not married to each other has been called a lot of names. Some states still use the term "bastard." Other words and phrases, less charged with condemnation, have been used to describe the illegitimate child: "out-of-wedlock child," "natural child," "child born outside of marriage," and even "love child." But these are either cumbersome or "camp." The word "illegitimate" means unlawful. Although the child has done no wrong, he is made illegitimate—unlawful—by virtue of his parents' unwed status. Although it may be harsh, the word "illegitimate" is used here because it is a reminder of how the child is viewed by others.

What Is an Illegitimate Child?

An illegitimate child is a child who is born to parents who are not married to each other. There is one exception: if a child is born to a woman who is married but the father is not her husband, there is a presumption of legitimacy, but it can be rebutted by the father, the mother, the husband, or eventually, the child.

Even if the child is wanted, he/she is considered illegitimate in the eyes of the law (and perhaps the community).[2]

Historically, some illegitimates fared better than others. In the civil-law countries, a distinction was made between children born to prostitutes and children born to mistresses.[3] The former could never be legitimated and were viewed as the dross of society. The latter could be legitimated by the subsequent intermarriage of their parents, and the father owed the child a duty of support. The distinction is retained in a slightly different form in Louisiana, which has its legal origins in the civil law. (See "How Can You Legitimate Your Illegitimate Child?" below.)

The English common law made no such distinction. A bastard was a bastard was a bastard and had no rights whatsoever—including no right to a name, no right to support from either father or mother, and no opportunity for legitimation, not even by adoption.

How Can You Legitimate Your Illegitimate Child?

Legitimation is the process by which an illegitimate child acquires most, but not necessarily all, of the legal rights possessed by legitimate children. For example, the child becomes entitled to his/her father's support and surname; he/she may inherit from either mother or father; he/she may get the fact of illegitimate birth erased from his/her birth records. But legitimation does not necessarily give the child the right to inherit in intestacy from his/her father's kin. In many states, there is no way that that can be accomplished.

Legitimation is not the same as acknowledgment or adjudication of paternity. An acknowledgment is basically an indication by a man that he is the father of a certain child. An adjudication of paternity is the conclusion by a court that a man is the father of a certain child. The procedure for legitimation varies from state to state. Some states require acknowledgment, some require adjudication, some require intermarriage, some require a combination of two of the three for the child to be legitimated.

In Arizona, North Dakota, and Puerto Rico, all children are declared legitimate and have the rights of legitimate children, so there is no need to legitimate a child. However, a problem arises where the father's identity is unclear or contested; regardless of what the law says, a child born out of wedlock has the same rights as a legitimate child only if his/her parents have been ascertained. In effect, there must be some proof of parentage for children born out of wedlock to have the rights of legitimate children in these places.

In twenty-three states you can legitimate your child by marrying each other before or after the child's birth.[4]

In sixteen states, a child is legitimated by the intermarriage of his/her parents *and* acknowledgment by the father.[5] Sometimes acknowledgment is required to be in writing and witnessed. In California, it is enough for the father to accept the child into his home; that constitutes acknowledgment by behavior. In Nebraska, the parents must have married each other and have had *other* children besides the child being legitimated; why is anybody's guess.

In nineteen states and the Virgin Islands, mere acknowledgment by the father legitimates the child.[6] In fifteen states and the Virgin Islands, a child may be legitimated by a court adjudication of paternity.[7] In Delaware and Massachusetts, a child may be legitimated by marriage between his/her parents *and* a court adjudication of paternity. In Maine, Maryland, Montana, Nebraska, Oklahoma, and Washington, D.C., a child may be legitimated by adoption by his/her natural parents.

Louisiana law is unique. An illegitimate child may be legitimated *only* if his/her parents were capable of marriage at the time of conception. They were capable of marriage if they were not relatives or not married to other people at the time of conception. If they were capable of marriage, the child is legitimated if they marry each other or the father acknowledges the child.

Keep in mind that legitimation means that the child can inherit from his/her parents if either should die without a will. But it does not necessarily mean that the child can inherit from the father's kin if one of them should die without a will.

Can an Illegitimate Child Inherit from His/Her Mother if She Dies without a Will?

Yes. The single exception is Louisiana. There, an illegitimate child can inherit from the mother only if she acknowledges the child and leaves no legitimate descendants. If the mother has legitimate descendants, the illegitimate child can inherit only enough for his/her support.[8]

Historically, an illegitimate child could not inherit from his/her mother. The child was considered *filius nullius,* or child of no one.

There is still some question in certain states whether the child can inherit from the mother's kin, since the statutes are often silent about it. Where the statute says the child is to its mother "as if legitimate," probably the mother's kin are included.

Otherwise case law will be determinative. No statutes expressly exclude the child from inheriting from the mother's kin. But in Mississippi, the illegitimate child can inherit from the mother's kin only if there are no legitimate heirs.

If inheritance from the mother's kin is allowed, the illegitimate child will generally inherit what the mother would have inherited if she had outlived her kin.

Can an Illegitimate Child Inherit from His/Her Father if He Dies without a Will?

This is one of the biggest issues in the law of illegitimacy. The answer varies from state to state. It depends on state statutes concerning intestate succession. Only a few jurisdictions allow the child to inherit from its father on the basis of the establishment of paternity alone.[9] The remaining states require that the child be legitimated. As has been discussed, that means anything from marrying the mother to acknowledgment, adjudication of paternity, or some combination. The requirement of legitimation is designed to protect the father from fraudulent claims against his estate. But the requirements of legitimation are often stricter than they need be. The mere fact of paternity is all that is necessary for a legitimate child to inherit from his/her father. Yet the illegitimate child has to show more of a connection than that: to wit, signed, notarized, witnessed, written statements of acknowledgment or a court decree and/or marriage between his parents. Few people have the energy or the foresight to go through these formalities, with the result that the illegitimate child suffers.

As of this writing the Supreme Court has agreed to review the Illinois law under which an illegitimate child cannot inherit from his/her father in intestacy unless the parents marry and the father acknowledges the child as his. The lower court upheld the law.[10] Despite the seeming inequity, the U.S. Supreme Court upheld the Louisiana law that allowed an acknowledged illegitimate child to inherit from his/her father only if the father left no other relations.[11] In that case, Rita Vincent was born to Lou Bertha Patterson and Ezra Vincent in March 1962. Two months later, Ezra signed a form before a notary stating that he was Rita's natural father. Rita and her parents lived together until Ezra died, without a will, in 1968. Rita claimed that as his child she should inherit from him. His other relatives also claimed the inheritance. The Louisiana law said that an illegitimate child may inherit from his/her father if he/she has been acknowledged provided that the father leaves no relatives. If the father leaves relatives, the illegitimate child may inherit only if he/she has been acknowledged *and* the father and mother have married each other. Rita's father's acknowledgment was not sufficient for her to be able to inherit from him. All the relatives got his property.

Rita argued that the statute discriminated against her in violation of the equal-protection clause of the Fourteenth Amendment just because she was illegitimate. There was no doubt Ezra was her father. Yet she was treated differently from legitimate off-spring. Nevertheless, the Court said that no prior cases say that a state can never treat an illegitimate child differently from legitimate offspring. It said that Louisiana had the power to make rules regarding descent and distribution of property; that the law had a rational basis in view of Louisiana's interest in promoting family life and in directing disposition of property within the state; and that the law posed no insurmountable barriers, since Rita's father could have legitimated her or made a will.

The dissent pointed out that the issue was not whether Louisiana had the power to make laws concerning intestate succession, but rather whether the law it *made* unlawfully discriminated against illegitimate children. The dissent claimed that it did, because there was no rational basis for distinguishing between acknowledged illegitimate and legitimate children:

> "Distinctions between citizens solely because of their ancestry are by their very nature odious to a free people whose institutions are founded upon the doctrine of equality." . . . The state court below explicitly upheld the statute on the ground that the punishment of the child might encourage the parents to marry. If that is the State's objective, it can obviously be attained far more directly by focusing on the parents whose actions the State seeks to influence. Given the importance and nature of the decision to marry . . . , I think that disinheriting the illegitimate child must be held to "bear no intelligible proper relation to the consequences that are made to flow" from the State's classification. . . .[12]

Therefore, as it stands now, you must *legitimate* your child in the precise manner required by your state to ensure that he/she will inherit from the father if the father dies without a will.

In states that permit an "acknowledged" illegitimate child to inherit from his/her father (unlike Louisiana), there is always the question of what constitutes acknowledgment. In some states, behavior is enough—supporting the child in your home—or oral or written statements that indicate you recognize the child as your own—a letter, for example. Other states specify something more formal—a signed, notarized, witnessed statement that the child is yours, on file with the county clerk. A Florida court recently held that an affidavit before a notary public that acknowledged the child and a birth certificate subsequently issued with the father's surname and signature were adequate.[13] But you should check the specific requirements of your state.

A few states have taken an interesting approach to whether the father and his kin can inherit from an illegitimate child.[14] They allow it only if the father has openly recognized the child and has not refused to support him/her. So even if a father legitimates his child, he may not be able to inherit from him/her.

Can the Problem of Inheritance Be Solved by Making a Will?

In most states, yes. You may bequeath your property to your illegitimate child; he/she may bequeath to you. However, in Louisiana, the parents of an illegitimate child may not bequeath him/her more than what is necessary for sustenance or to provide an occupation if either leaves legitimate descendants as well.[15]

If You Say "My Child" in Your Will, Is It Sufficient to Designate Your Illegitimate Child?

Not usually. Saying "to my child" will be sufficient if the illegitimate child is your only child and if your relationship is established. It is better to say "I give my Alfa Romeo to Nina Starr, who is my daughter." That way it is clear that you mean the person, and the relationship is merely descriptive.

Who Has the Obligation to Support an Illegitimate Child?

At common law, an illegitimate child had no right to support.[16] His/her maintenance fell upon the parish. Today an illegitimate child has the same right to support from his/her biological parents as a legitimate child. Generally speaking, the father has the primary and the mother the secondary obligation to support the child.[17] This is consistent with prevalent although increasingly outmoded notions that the male should be the breadwinner. Of course, the ability to obtain support from the father depends upon whether his paternity can be ascertained.

Traditionally, this is done by a paternity suit. The mother, child, or guardian of the child may bring a suit—usually in family court—to establish the paternity of a child.

In What Style Is an Illegitimate Child Required to Be Supported?

A legitimate child is required to be supported according to his or her father's *means*. An illegitimate child is required to be supported to the minimum extent of his or her *needs*. The definition of "needs" is usually up to the judge. Once paternity has been established, there seems to be no reason for treating illegitimate and legitimate children differently. Yet this discrimination persists.

Can the Mother of an Illegitimate Child Be Required to Reveal the Child's Paternity as a Condition for Eligibility for Aid to Families with Dependent Children (AFDC) Welfare Benefits?

Yes. Many state statutes and now Section 402 of the Social Security Act require unwed mothers to disclose the name of the father and to cooperate in a paternity action against him as a condition for aid.

The rule was challenged in federal court as an invasion of the mother's privacy. But the court held that the disclosure requirement does not invade her privacy because she has already revealed her unwed status. It was also challenged on the theory that it imposes an irrebuttable presumption that disclosure is in the best interests of the child, a presumption that is unjustified. The court, however, held that the statute presents no irrebuttable presumption but is "instead a legislative value judgment about the responsibility, financial and perhaps moral, of all fathers."[18]

Ironically, without considering the constitutional

arguments, the Supreme Court has held that the New York law that required AFDC recipients to cooperate in paternity suits against absent parents as a condition for eligibility was invalid as being against the Social Security Act.[19] Just as the case was decided, however, the Social Security Act was amended to include such a provision, so the two were no longer inconsistent.

Will an Agreement to Support Your Illegitimate Child Be Enforced?

Yes, although the court will do what it feels is "in the best interest of the child," keeping in mind that the father has the primary and the mother the secondary obligation to support the child. A support agreement between the parents of an illegitimate child would be significant proof of paternity in a paternity suit.

What Is the Legal Name of an Illegitimate Child?

At common law, an illegitimate child acquired his/her name by repute. He/she was not entitled to either the father's or the mother's name. Nearly the same situation prevails today, although at least one court has said that the illegitimate child has a right to his mother's surname.[20] But the illegitimate child cannot compel his/her father to let him/her use the father's surname without an order establishing paternity.

At common law, the father has the exclusive right to determine the surname of a legitimate child and

the mother has the right to determine the surname
of an illegitimate child. This situation still prevails.
Neither parent has to choose his or her own surname but can choose any name he/she wants as
long as it is not used for any fraudulent purpose. So
an illegitimate child may be given his father's name
if the father agrees, but the father has no right to
require that the child take his name.[21] (See also the
discussion of acquiring a name by repute, pages
160–161.)

Ordinarily, if a married woman has a child by a
man who is not her husband, her husband would
still have the right to name the child. But a recent
Pennsylvania attorney general's opinion says that a
child of a married woman may be given the surname
of a man, not her husband, who is the father if (1)
the natural father acknowledges paternity, (2) she
acknowledges the natural father, and (3) the
mother's husband gives permission.[22]

Who Is Entitled to Custody of an Illegitimate Child?

Until very recently, there was no recognition that the
father of an illegitimate child may have an interest
in the welfare of his children, much less a right to
their custody. Before that time, several states provided that if a "parent" was unfit, the child would
become a ward of the state. The "parent" would be
entitled to a hearing regarding his/her fitness. "Parent" meant the mother and father of a legitimate child
and the mother of an illegitimate child. But it did
not include the father of an illegitimate child. This
was true in Illinois. For eighteen years, Peter and
Joan Stanley lived together and had three children.

Peter supported the children and they lived as a family. When Joan died, the state put the children up for adoption without asking Peter's permission and without determining his fitness to care for them. Peter sued the state, claiming that the Illinois law denied him equal protection, since married fathers and unwed mothers could not be deprived of their children without a showing that they were unfit. The U.S. Supreme Court held in *Stanley* v. *Illinois* that as a matter of due process, Peter Stanley was entitled to a hearing on his fitness before he could be deprived of his children.[23] He got his children back and in doing so began a shake-up in the law concerning the rights of the father of illegitimate children.

Now the father of an illegitimate child is entitled to notice and a hearing before his child can be taken from him. The requirement may be difficult to fulfill where the father is unidentified or has taken flight. But it ensures the rights of those fathers of illegitimate children who do wish to care for them. The decision in *Stanley* acknowledges that such fathers exist and thereby helps to break down a stereotype. It signifies a revolution in the definition of fathering—from denoting a mere biological fact to denoting a continuous, responsible relationship with one's child.

As between the mother and father, however, a different situation exists. The mother is the preferred custodian and the father must generally show that she is unfit before he will be awarded custody. In theory, this differs from the law concerning the custody of legitimate children. There, the law puts mother and father on an equal basis. For example, the New York Domestic Relations Law, Section 70, says: "In all cases there shall be no prima facie right to the custody of the child in either parent, but the court shall determine solely what is for the best interests of the child and what will best promote its welfare and happiness." In practice, however, the mother is the preferred custodian of the legitimate child too, but this has more to do with tradition than with the mandate of law. As notions of proper sex roles change, the presumptions that the mother should be the preferred custodian and that fathers of illegitimate children are less concerned about them than are fathers of legitimate children will also have to change. As the Court said in *Stanley:* "It may be, as the State insists, that most unmarried fathers are unsuitable and neglectful parents. It may also be that Stanley is such a parent and that his children should be placed in other hands. But all unmarried fathers are not in this category; some are wholly suited to have custody of their children."[24]

What Are the Rights of the Father of an Illegitimate Child?

This is really a rather novel question. The father of an out-of-wedlock child has been traditionally billed as a love-'em-and-leave-'em type. He is supposed to demonstrate little concern for the woman he has impregnated and even less concern for the child. Most of the law concerning illegitimacy involves getting this rogue to shoulder his responsibility to support the child. So, in New York you have the paternity suit. The mother hauls the father into court pointing the finger at him—he's the one—he denying it all the way, dragging his friends into court to testify that they had intercourse with her around the same time too. A rather disturbing affair. If adequate proof is demonstrated, the judge issues an order of filiation—a court adjudication of paternity. From then on, the reluctant gentleman has an enforceable obligation to support the child. Three specific provisions of the New York law show the degree to which the father is presumed to be disinterested in his child. First, he is not among those who can bring a paternity suit. He does not have the authority to go to court to establish that he is the child's father—the scenario is that he goes reluctantly, that, in fact, he is the mother's adversary in a paternity proceeding. Second, the mother has the primary right of custody. If she wants the child and is "fit," she'll get custody. There is no theoretical presumption, as there is with legitimate children, that the parents have *equal* rights to custody. Third, the mother can give up the child for adoption without the consent of the father—she can act unilaterally; again, the presumption is that he doesn't care enough to be concerned about what happens to the child.

For years, people had been concerned with the obligations of the father. It is only recently that we have begun to discuss his *rights* and to consider that the father of an illegitimate child may wish to be known as the father, may accept the obligations of supporting his child, may wish to raise his child, and may wish to have a say in whether or not the child is given up for adoption.

So far, the only articulated right the father of an illegitimate child has is the right to a hearing on his fitness in a custody battle between him and the state. In other words, the state may not presume him to be unfit but must give him the opportunity to show that he is fit to have custody before the children are put in the custody of a state agency after the mother's death. Beyond this, there are still many open questions.

Can the Mother of an Illegitimate Child Give the Child Up for Adoption without the Father's Consent?

Yes. In New York State, which appears to be typical of most states on this issue, the mother has the statutory right to do so without the father's consent.[25] This statute appears to be contrary to the U.S. Supreme Court decision in *Stanley* v. *Illinois,* which recognized the natural father's right to a hearing on the issue of his own fitness to have custody and what course of action would be in the best interest of the child. But the courts are still far from implementing the reasoning in *Stanley*. The New York statute was recently upheld by the highest court of the state.

A man and woman who were living together had a child in 1970. They lived together for about another year and a half after the birth of the child. Then they separated. The father paid the rent on the mother and child's apartment; he willingly acknowledged his paternity in a paternity suit; he paid child support and visited the child regularly. The mother then married another man and her husband sought to adopt the child over the natural father's strenuous objections. Despite the fact that the father had demonstrated his interest in his child, the court held that he had no say in whether the child could be adopted by someone else. This was the sole right of the mother under the statute.[26]

Until courts begin to see that some fathers of illegitimate children *are* concerned about their children, these fathers will have great difficulty asserting the procedural rights accorded them, at least in spirit, by *Stanley*.

In addition to the reluctance of courts to implement the spirit of *Stanley,* a concerned father may face another hurdle in having a say in whether his children are adopted by or put in the custody of others; that is, he will have great difficulty asserting his right to a hearing if he cannot prove paternity.

That may occur if the mother dies and can't testify or if the mother does not know or does not wish to disclose who the father is. To establish paternity without the mother's cooperation, the man must be able to demonstrate that he has assumed parental obligations in relation to the child. The best thing is to get your name on the birth certificate as father, support the child (keep a record of this), take an active part in the child's life even if you do not have custody, see the child's teachers, sign the report cards, and so on.

Can a Single Person Adopt a Child?

Yes, technically. But there are subtle barriers to adoption by a single person and they are compounded when you are living with someone. Every adoption must be approved by a court. In evaluating your fitness to adopt, the court looks for the traditional two-parent family—so single people are second-best—and for evidence of "moral" fitness. Whether you will be declared fit to adopt depends on the judge's attitude toward sex and his perception of community standards.

It is doubtful that both of you can adopt the same child if you are living together. New York State Domestic Relation Law, Section 110, which is probably typical, reads: "*An* adult unmarried person or an adult husband and his adult wife together may adopt another person" (emphasis added). This indicates that only one of you may adopt the child.

Can an Illegitimate Child Recover for the Wrongful Death of His/Her Mother? Father? Can a Parent Recover for the Wrongful Death of His/Her Illegitimate Child?

This issue came to the fore in 1968 in *Levy* v. *Louisiana*.[27] There, the Supreme Court held that unacknowledged illegitimate children could maintain an action for the wrongful death of their mother. Then, in *Glona* v. *American Guarantee and Liability Insurance Company,* the Supreme Court held that the mother of an illegitimate child could sue for his wrongful death.[28] In both cases, the state argued that denying benefits to and from illegitimate children discouraged illegitimacy and sin. Yet in *Glona,* the Court said: "It would indeed be farfetched to assume that women have illegitimate children so that they can be compensated for their death."[29]

These cases presumably establish also an illegitimate child's right to recover for the wrongful death of a father and the father's right to recover for the wrongful death of an illegitimate child. The problem, however, again hinges on proof—is this man the father of this child?

Can an Illegitimate Child Recover under State Workmen's Compensation Statutes for the Death of, or Injury to, His Father?

Yes. In 1972, in *Weber* v. *Aetna Casualty and Surety Co. et al.*, the Supreme Court held that an unacknowledged illegitimate child could recover.[30] Here again, the Court said: "Nor can it be thought here that persons will shun illicit relations because the offspring may not one day reap the benefits of workmen's compensation."[31]

This case was especially poignant. Henry Stokes's wife was in a mental hospital. He lived with Willie Mae Weber, their (illegitimate) child, and Henry's four children by his wife. Since Henry was already married, he could not have married Willie Mae without procuring a divorce. Stokes was killed in an employment-related accident. Willie Mae was pregnant with their second child, which was born after Henry's death. Under Louisiana law, the four legitimate children could recover his workmen's compensation benefits, but the two illegitimate children could not. The Court struck down the statute and allowed the two illegitimate children to recover. It said:

> The status of illegitimacy has expressed through the ages society's condemnation of irresponsible liaisons beyond the bonds of marriage. But visiting this condemnation on the head of an infant is illogical and

unjust. Moreover, imposing disabilities on the illegitimate child is contrary to the basic concept of our system that legal burdens should bear some relationship to individual responsibility or wrongdoing. Obviously, no child is responsible for his birth and penalizing the illegitimate child is an ineffectual—as well as unjust—way of deterring the parent. . . .[32]

Again, the problem is one of proof of paternity.

Can an Illegitimate Child Recover as Beneficiary of His/Her Father's Social Security Benefits?

Yes. Ramon Jimenez was living with Elizabeth Hernandez and their three children. He acknowledged them, but under Illinois law this was not enough to legitimate them. Ramon became disabled. Under the Social Security Act at that time, an illegitimate child was entitled to benefits if the state law allowed him/her to inherit in intestacy. But the Illinois law did not permit children who were not legitimate to do so. So the Hernandez-Jimenez children received no benefits. The case went to the Supreme Court and the court said that they should be entitled to benefits, since the law discriminated against them merely because of their status of birth, a classification justified by no legitimate state interest.[33] Again, the remaining problem is proof of paternity.

Can an Illegitimate Child Recover as a "Child" under Various Other Federal Benefit Programs?

Federal benefit programs fall into three categories: (1) ones that allow the illegitimate child to recover if there is proof of paternity, e.g., the Social Security Act and the Veterans Administration Act; (2) ones that include illegitimate children in the definition of "child," e.g., the Federal Employers' Liability Act; and (3) ones that rely for the definition of "child" on a state-law determination of who is entitled to inherit if the parent dies without a will, e.g., the Federal Employees' Group Life Insurance Act and the Copyright Act.

Under the first two categories, recovery is virtually assured the illegitimate child, assuming he/she can prove paternity. In the third category, however, recovery may be difficult, since state laws, as we have seen, have extensive and varying requirements for legitimation for purposes of intestate succession.

It is difficult to understand why some federal benefits are extended to illegitimates and not others. Most likely the patchwork reflects the varying degree of concern about the problem of establishing paternity felt by the authors and interpreters of the laws. In addition, the statutes are more likely to include illegitimates where their purpose is compensatory than where their purpose is to determine how to distribute property.

While there has been a liberalization, keep in mind that if you want your illegitimate child to have all the benefits of a legitimate child, you must conform to the state procedures for legitimation—i.e., whatever your state requires for an illegitimate child to inherit in intestacy.

Can an Illegitimate Child Sue His/Her Alleged Father or His/Her Mother for "Wrongful Life"?

A child does not ask to be born. Should he/she be able to hold his/her parents accountable for bringing him/her into a world that is hostile by virtue of the fact that his/her parents are not married?

Most courts have not had to address this question. The Appellate Court of Illinois has said no. The court felt it could not create such a cause of action because it would open the door to too many suits— not only by illegitimates: "One might seek damages for being born of a certain color, another because of race; one for being born with a hereditary disease, another for inheriting unfortunate family characteristics; one for being born into a large and destitute family, another because a parent has an unsavory reputation."[34] In keeping with that decision, it seems reasonable to predict that the law will move in the direction of improving the status of the illegitimate child rather than compensating him/her for his/her low status in the eyes of society.

Is an Illegitimate Child Born Abroad to an American Father and a Non-American Mother a U.S. Citizen?

No, unless the child is legitimated by the father before the child reaches twenty-one.[35] Yet the illegitimate child of an American mother by a non-American father has U.S. citizenship without legitimation.[36]

The higher standard for men no doubt reflects the attitude that "our boys" abroad should be able to impregnate local women with impunity, or at least that they should be insulated from unfounded allegations of paternity. However, the equitable approach to determine citizenship would be to require establishment of paternity, not the technicality of legitimation. Foreign-born children of Americans should be entitled to U.S. citizenship whether or not the parents care enough to legitimate them.

Is There a Tax Disadvantage to Being an Illegitimate Child or to Having One?

Yes. Most state inheritance and gift tax laws give a break to bequests or gifts to "children." The definition of "children" does not include illegitimates. So neither you nor your child benefits from these privileges.

NOTES

1. Jessie Bernard, *The Future of Marriage* (New York: World Publishers, 1972), p. 57.

2. In 1973, about 13 percent of live births in the United States were illegitimate children, an increase from 3.9 percent in 1950, 5.3 percent in 1960, and 10.7 percent in 1970. About 53 percent were born to women under twenty years old and 82 percent to women under twenty-five. Data from U.S. Bureau

of the Census, *Statistical Abstract of the United States: 1975*, 96th ed. (Washington, D.C., 1975), Table 77, "Illegitimate Live Births, by Race and Age of Mother: 1950–1973."

3. In countries with a civil-law system (France, Italy, Spain), the laws are set forth in codes. In countries with a common-law system (Great Britain, United States), the laws are set forth not only in codes, but also in judicial decisions.

4. Alaska, Arkansas, Colorado, Connecticut, Florida, Hawaii, Idaho, Kentucky, Maine, Michigan, Minnesota, Missouri, Nevada, New Mexico, New York, Pennsylvania, South Carolina, South Dakota, Tennessee, Texas, Virginia, Washington, West Virginia.

5. Alabama, California, Delaware, Georgia, Illinois, Indiana, Louisiana, Maryland, Massachusetts, Mississippi, Nebraska, New Hampshire, New Jersey, Ohio, Rhode Island, Wyoming.

6. Alabama, Alaska, Delaware, Iowa, Kansas, Maine, Maryland, Montana, Nebraska, Nevada, New Mexico, North Carolina, Oklahoma, Oregon, Utah, Vermont, Virginia, Washington, Wisconsin.

7. Alaska, Colorado, Florida, Idaho, Indiana, Iowa, Kansas, Maryland, Minnesota, New York, North Carolina, Oregon, South Dakota, Vermont, Wisconsin.

8. Louisiana Statutes Annotated, C.C. Art. 918 (West 1952).

9. Arizona, North Dakota, and Puerto Rico.

10. *Trimble* v. *Gordon*, appeal to U.S. Supreme Court docketed March 22, 1976, Docket No. 75–5952.

11. *Labine* v. *Vincent*, 401 U.S. 532 (1970).

12. *Ibid.*, p. 558, footnote omitted.

13. *Locke* v. *Campbell's Estate*, Fla. App., 305 So. 2d 825 (1975).

14. Alaska, Colorado, Idaho, South Dakota.

15. Louisiana Statutes Annotated, C.C. Art. 1483 (West 1952).

16. Common law refers to legal principles developed in early English history. It also refers to judicial decisions in the United States that are based on those principles.

17. The obligation of the father to support his illegitimate child was established in *Gomez* v. *Perez,* 409 U.S. 535 (1973).

18. *Doe* v. *Norton,* 365 F. Supp. 65, 74, 75 (D. Conn. 1973).

19. *Lascaris* v. *Shirley,* 420 U.S. 730 (1975); see also *Doe* v. *Norton,* 422 U.S. 391 (1975).

20. *Buckley* v. *State,* 19 Ala. App. 508, 98 So. 362 (1923).

21. See Wisconsin Attorney General's Opinion, 1 Family Law Reporter 2134.

22. See Pennsylvania Attorney General's Opinion, 1 Family Law Reporter 2320.

23. *Stanley* v. *Illinois,* 405 U.S. 645 (1972).

24. *Ibid.,* p. 654.

25. N.Y.S. Domestic Relations Law § 111 (McKinney's 1964).

26. *Matter of Malpica-Orsini,* 36 N.Y.2d 568, 370 N.Y.S.2d 511, 331 N.E.2d 486 (1975).

27. *Levy* v. *Louisiana,* 391 U.S. 68 (1968).

28. *Glona* v. *American Guarantee and Liability Insurance Company,* 391 U.S. 73 (1968).

29. *Ibid.,* p. 75.

30. *Weber* v. *Aetna Casualty & Surety Company et al.,* 406 U.S. 164 (1972).

31. *Ibid.,* p. 173.

32. *Ibid.,* p. 175.

33. *Jimenez* v. *Weinberger,* 417 U.S. 628 (1974).

34. *Zepeda* v. *Zepeda*, 41 Ill. App. 2d 240, 190 N.E.2d 849 (1963).

35. Nationality Act of 1940, 8 U.S.C. § 1409(a), 1970.

36. *Ibid.*, § 1409(c).

5 / Property

Karen's mother always told her to get married because "if he leaves you, you can always get alimony." Her advice reflects the view of marriage as an economic relationship. Indeed, that is a great part of what marriage is. Not surprisingly, the laws of marriage are primarily concerned with property: who owns what, who manages it, who gets it on breaking up, how does it pass from generation to generation. And, it is thought, the laws of marriage protect women and ensure that they are provided for. But do they really?

Even where alimony is awarded, it is not always collected. And the fact that the husband has the primary obligation to support the wife creates a subtle bias against hiring married women or paying them well. In addition, some states still do not permit a married woman to manage, sell, or mortgage property without her husband's consent.

The relationships between people who are living together and those who are married are factually similar. But are they treated similarly by the law? No. Married people have their choices made for them by the state. If you are living together, you can obtain most (but not all) of the benefits of marriage through wills and contracts. However, remember that eternal vigilance is the price of liberty.

Any discussion of how the law affects the property of people living together must begin with a clarification of some legal concepts.

What Kinds of Property Are There?

There are two kinds of property: real property and personal property. Real property means land, buildings, fixtures (property that is affixed to land with the intention of increasing its usefulness or value—e.g., an oil burner), and sometimes crops, trees, and bushes. Personal property means movable objects like furniture, clothing, automobiles. It may also be intangible, like money in a bank account or stocks and bonds.

Why Is the Distinction between Real and Personal Property Important?

It is important because the requirements for acquisition of each kind of property vary. For example, a contract to purchase real property must be in writing, but a contract to purchase personal property need not always be in writing. There may also be presumptions as to who owns the property depending on whether it is real or personal. For example, a gift of real property to a husband and wife is presumed by New York State law to be to them as tenants by the entirety (see below). A gift to them of personal property is presumed to be owned as tenants in common (see below). Therefore, determining the kind of property may help in determining who owns it or what procedure one must follow in order to own it.

How May Property Be Owned?

The law recognizes single ownership and three types of joint ownership: people can own property (1) as tenants by the entirety, (2) as joint tenants, or (3) as tenants in common. (The word "tenant" dates from feudal times and is derived from the Latin word meaning to "hold." A person could not own land but could only hold an interest in land. This interest determined his relationship to the monarch, which was called "tenure"; he was called a "tenant." Today, the word "tenant" applies to ownership of both real and personal property.)

What Is Tenancy by the Entirety?

Tenancy by the entirety is a kind of joint ownership peculiar to married couples. It applies to real property only. In tenancy by the entirety, neither husband nor wife may sell or give away any part of the property without the other's consent. If one dies, the other automatically inherits.

What Is Joint Tenancy?

Joint tenancy applies to real and personal property. You do not have to be married to be joint tenants, although you may be. If one owner dies, the other(s) inherit(s) his/her share automatically. Unlike tenants by the entirety, however, each joint tenant may individually sell or give away his/her share of the property without the consent of the other(s). But if one of them does that, the joint tenancy ceases and the owners become tenants in common. Joint tenants need not have equal shares in the property.

What Is Tenancy in Common?

Tenancy in common also applies to both real and personal property. Each owner has an interest in the property. These interests need not be equal but are determined by the amount each contributes to the purchase price. Unlike tenancy by the entirety or joint tenancy, if a tenant in common dies, the other tenants in common do *not* automatically inherit his/her share. Instead, the share passes through the estate of the deceased to the beneficiaries under his/her will or to his/her statutorily determined heirs if there is no will.

Why Are the Types of Ownership Important?

The types of ownership are important because each has a different effect on whether you can sell or give away the property and what happens to it on the death of one of the owners or on the dissolution of the relationship. In addition, we see that the type of ownership one may enjoy is linked to marital status. Only spouses are permitted to own property in such a way that they may prevent each other from selling or giving it away. Historically, the tenancy by the entirety was probably meant to function as a check on the husband to insure that if he died the wife would be left with something. But she had to relinquish her rights to own or manage property *during* the marriage. So it was by no means an equal trade off. Today, since married women in most states may own and manage property, the tenancy by the entirety simply functions as a mutual check. Most lawyers automatically draw up the deed as tenants by the entirety when a married couple buys real property. If there is a divorce, the tenancy by the entirety is converted to a tenancy in common.

Are There Different Marital Property Systems in the United States?

Yes. The two marital property systems followed in the United States are the "separate" and the "community" property systems. The separate property system is derived from English common law. The community property system is derived from French and Spanish civil law. Eight states follow the community property system—Arizona, California, Idaho, Louisiana, Nevada, New Mexico, Texas, and Washington. The other states follow the separate property system.

What Is the Community Property System?

The basic principle of the community property system is that all property acquired during the marriage belongs equally to the husband and the wife unless they provide otherwise by contract. If the marriage dissolves, either by death or divorce, each spouse, or the spouse's estate, is entitled to one half of the property. Whether this principle will apply to your marriage depends not on where you marry but on where you are domiciled at the time of dissolution. (See Chapter 11.)

Who has the right to manage and control community property? In other words, who decides what a family buys and what it sells? Originally, in all the community property states, the husband was accorded the exclusive right to manage and control community property. This is still the ironclad rule in Louisiana, where the statute designates the husband as the "head and master of the community of gains" during the marriage.[1] Within the last few years, as a response to increased concern about the rights of women, the seven other community property states have adopted the principle of joint management by husband and wife.[2] This principle has the effect of requiring both spouses, for example, to consent to convey real property or to incur a debt.

What Is the Separate Property System?

Under the separate property system, each spouse owns his/her property separately. Although the spouses may agree to own property jointly, the presumption is that whoever pays for it, is given it, or has title to it owns it. On dissolution, whoever has title to the property or shows that he or she acquired it through payment or gift owns it. This system may work to the detriment of a spouse who does not work outside the home or is not independently wealthy. At the end of the marriage, what does such a spouse own?

What Is the Primary Difference between the Community Property and Separate Property Systems?

The primary difference is that the community property system compensates a spouse who has not worked outside the home for labor in the home when the marriage ends whether because of divorce or death. The separate property system does not recognize the value of such a spouse's contribution.

Of course, states with separate property systems have attempted to devise methods of protecting a spouse who has not worked outside the home. First, joint ownership of certain property, like the residence, is common. So upon dissolution, even though a spouse who had not worked outside the home had not paid for the asset, he/she would have an interest in it. The person who had paid for the asset would be considered to have made a gift of an interest in the asset to the spouse who had not worked outside the home. Second, legislatures have provided that although in a divorce proceeding the court may not change *title* of property from one spouse to another, it may decide who should get *possession* of the property.[3] Third, legislatures have provided that a spouse has the right to elect against the deceased spouse's will. This means that regardless of what the will provides, the spouse may assert his/her right to a share determined by the statute.[4] Despite these methods, however, a spouse who has not worked outside the home is not guaranteed economic security upon dissolution of the marriage. He/she will be at the mercy of some court's discretion.

If Two People Who Are Living Together Acquire Property, to Whom Does It Belong?

This is a question they can and should determine when they acquire it, although their decision may be modified at any time. Single people, whether living with another or not, can own property in three of the four ways outlined before: separately, as joint tenants, or as tenants in common. What is most important is clarity of ownership. If it is left unclear, and a conflict arises, a court will decide who owns what and not always to the satisfaction of both parties. The main thing the judge will consider is who has title to the property, not who needs it more, which may be considered when a couple is married. The judge may find that the person with title holds the property for another who is the intended owner, but that is done only when unusual inequity would otherwise result. (See resulting trust, page 83.) Clarity of ownership is important also because ownership leads to obligations. For example, the owner is liable for injuries occurring on his real property or by reason of his personal property. He is liable for real property taxes, registration of a motor vehicle, and so on. The time of acquisition is a good one for clarifying ownership because the parties are still communicating. The ideal way to clarify ownership is to put title to the property in the name of the person(s) who the parties agree should take possession of the property if their relationship ceases. If this is not possible, the two people should make a written agreement, but this agreement must be carefully drafted or a court will not enforce it.

What Factors Should People Who Are Living Together Consider in Deciding Who Takes Title to Real Property?

Clarity of ownership is a relatively simple matter with real property because contracts of sale must be in writing and there are deeds. Let us suppose Carl and Karen are buying a house. They will be as tempted as others to adjust title according to numerous supposedly money-saving schemes. For example, if they intend to rent the house for part of the year, the high earner will be tempted to put title in the low earner's name to avoid increased taxable income. The person with a high risk in business will be tempted to put title in the person with a low risk to avoid the possibility of creditors' reaching the asset. Both will be tempted to put title in the one with the better credit rating to facilitate the purchase. These are all real considerations. But while these kinds of strategies may work with married persons because the state lends its hand in adjusting rights upon dissolution, they may not work with unmarried people. The considerations unmarried people living together must keep foremost in their minds are who gets the property if they break up and how does each of them protect his/her interest in the property?

If Carl and Karen separate, a court will award

possession of the house to the person with title. It will only deviate from this presumption if the person who does not hold title can prove that he/she contributed a specific portion of the purchase price. This is known as a resulting trust. The titleholder is considered to be the trustee of the person who does not hold title to the extent of the latter's contribution. Resulting trust is extremely difficult to prove. (See page 96 for some relevant court cases.)

Separate ownership is recommended only if one of the parties puts up all the money. Problems arise where one person provides the money, but both agree that they wish to take title jointly. For example, suppose Carl and Karen take title jointly, agreeing that he will supply the money and she will do housekeeping for five years. If they were to decide to separate after the third year and Carl sought to claim the house as his alone, a court would refuse to enforce their agreement but would probably say that Carl had made a gift to Karen of one half the value of the house—the presumption of ownership by the titleholder(s) is that strong. But that leaves Carl in a difficult position.

If, as is the case with most people, Carl and Karen have each contributed part of the purchase price, each will wish to protect his/her equity. Either joint tenancy or tenancy in common would make sense. Whether they take title as joint tenants or tenants in common depends on whether they wish each other to have the right of survivorship. Joint tenants inherit the property from each other automatically; tenants in common do not. If either Carl or Karen is married to someone else, they must keep in mind that the spouse has first claim on the property (known as the right of election) if the one who is married should die. In addition, upon the death of a joint tenant, the entire value of the property is included in his/her estate for tax purposes unless the other joint tenant can prove some contribution to the purchase price. The value included in the estate is reduced to the extent the surviving joint tenant can prove contribution. But if no contribution is proved, one person's estate may be subject to tax for the entire value of the property. If the property is owned by tenancy in common, there is no automatic right of survivorship and Carl and Karen must provide for each other by will if they wish. If they separate, each takes one half the house or one half the value of the proceeds.

What Factors Should People Who Are Living Together Consider in Deciding Who Owns Personal Property?

Clarity of ownership of personal property is difficult to establish because deeds are not required and not all contracts of purchase must be in writing. In addition, where personal property is used in common—for example, household furniture—the view of who owns what may become blurred over time, and Carl and Karen may find they have very different ideas by the time a breakup occurs. If there is a dispute, the court would award the property to the person who paid for it. That can be shown by canceled check, receipt, contract of sale, credit card bills, and the like. Other factors may also be considered, such as for whom was the item purchased, by whom was it intended to be used, in whose name is it registered (e.g., a car), was a gift made? Note that if the parties were married, the court would not necessarily award the property to the person who paid for it. In a separate property state, although title may rest in the husband in the sense that he paid for the item, the court could grant possession to the wife. In a community property state, objects used in common are marital property and one half would go to each spouse.

So Carl and Karen should consider buying separately personal property that will be used in common. Whether they buy separately or jointly, they should keep their receipts. They might wish to make a written agreement specifying who gets what in the event of a breakup, but as will be discussed, this agreement must be carefully drafted in order to be enforceable.

Can an Owner Legally Refuse to Sell His/Her Property to an Unmarried Couple? Can He/She Refuse to Put Both Names on the Deed/

Yes. An owner can sell his property to whoever he pleases. Two people who are living together do not have any recognized rights to buy, for example, a house or cooperative apartment together. One legitimate reason why a seller may not wish to sell to you is out of a fear that if you split up he/she will have to chase both of you to collect whatever is owed him/her because neither of you is responsible for the other's obligations.

The only limits on a seller's right to choose his/her buyer are federal, state, and local fair housing laws that prohibit discrimination in the sale of housing on the basis of race, religion, national origin, sex, and in a few cases, marital status. There are four states—Delaware, Minnesota, New Jersey, and Oregon—that prohibit such discrimination on the basis of marital status.[5] The New York City Administrative Code does so as well.[6] These provisions were designed to get at the problem of homeowners' refusing to sell to individuals because they were *single*. Presumably, single people are less reliable than married people; they lead fast lives—full of sex, drugs, alcohol, and loud parties lasting until 4 A.M. If you are denied housing because you are living together, you may try to sue the seller under one of these statutes. The issue for unmarried couples is whether the statutes prohibiting discrimination in housing on the basis of marital status apply to them. The question has not yet been asked or answered by a court or legislature. So these statutes do not yet give unmarried couples any protection.

If you are denied housing because you are an unmarried couple, you may also argue in court that this is a denial of credit on the basis of marital status. Such denial is illegal under the Federal Equal Credit Opportunity Act[7] and by statute in thirteen states.[8] The unmarried couple's problem in making this argument is twofold: is the sale of a home the granting of credit within the meaning of the statute, and does refusal to sell to an unmarried couple constitute discrimination on the basis of marital status?

An unmarried couple denied access to housing might also be able to invoke the equal-protection clause of the Fourteenth Amendment to the Constitution, which provides that no state shall deny to any person within its jurisdiction the equal protection of the laws. The major hurdle here is that you must show that a *state*, not a private entity like a club or business, is violating your rights. Therefore, you might be able to assert the equal-protection clause to obtain public housing (but it would be difficult to use it successfully to acquire a private home or apartment). You would have to argue that had you been married, you would have been permitted to take title to the property, but because you were unmarried, you were deprived of the right of all citizens to own property. Then you would have to show that there is no legitimate reason to make a distinction between married and unmarried couples.

As might be expected, you may have much more difficulty buying property together in a state in which fornication or cohabitation is a crime if you let on that you intend to live together, because the owner could be prosecuted for facilitating a crime. On the other hand, if you deceive the owner, and he/she thereby suffers monetary damage, you can be held liable for fraud.

Basically, no matter where you live, you have no recognized right to buy property together or to have both names put on the deed.

Can a Landlord Legally Refuse to Rent to Two People Because They Are Not Married to Each Other?

The answer to this question depends primarily upon whether cohabitation is illegal in the state in which the apartment is located. Cohabitation is illegal in twenty states and fornication—sexual intercourse between persons not married to each other—is illegal in sixteen states and Washington, D.C. (See

Table 1, page 33.) Although prosecutions are rarely brought under these statutes, the fact that they exist at all acts as an impediment to living together. While the statutes do not expressly make it illegal for a landlord to rent to unmarried people who wish to live together, it is conceivable that the landlord could be charged with facilitating a crime and, at least, he/she has the moral force of the statutes behind his/her refusal. Therefore in states where cohabitation and/or fornication are illegal, a landlord is in a strong legal position in refusing to rent to people who are not married to each other.

In states like New York, however, where there are no such statutes, a landlord would be doing nothing illegal in renting to people who are not married to each other. There is still, however, nothing to compel him/her to rent to you; he/she may legally refuse.

An allied question is whether you can be evicted for living together. In 1971, a New York State Civil Court judge was called upon to decide whether an unmarried woman could be evicted for having intercourse in her apartment. The judge ruled that "acts of sexual intercourse between unmarried consenting adults involving neither public disorder nor prostitution do not constitute a basis for eviction."[9] Thus, at least in New York, you cannot be evicted for having intercourse or, by analogy, for living together. However, in a state where cohabitation and fornication are illegal, living together would be grounds for eviction.

What Problems May Arise When One Person Moves in with the Other?

In this situation, the terms of the lease govern. Leases often provide that the apartment is for the use of the tenant and "immediate family" only. This clause bars a roommate and its violation is grounds for eviction. You cannot compel your landlord to accept the new tenant even if you agree to an increase in rent.

Can Zoning Ordinances Legally Prohibit Two Unmarried People from Living Together?

This specific question has not yet been answered by the Supreme Court, although the answer is probably no. The Court has, however, held that a zoning ordinance may prohibit *more* than two unrelated people from living together.

It is not unusual for a community to enact zoning ordinances that restrict housing to one-family occupancy. The definition of "family" is what may create problems for unmarried people living together. A zoning ordinance of the Village of Belle Terre, New York, defined "family" thus: "One or more persons related by blood, adoption or marriage, living and cooking together as a single housekeeping unit [or] . . . a number of persons but not exceeding two (2) living and cooking together as a single housekeeping unit though not related by blood, adoption, or marriage shall be deemed to constitute a family." Six unrelated male and female students at the State University of New York at Stony Brook rented a house in Belle Terre. In July 1972, the owners of

the house were notified that they would be subject
to a maximum $100 fine or a maximum of sixty
days in jail for violating the ordinance. Three of the
students and the owners sued the village officials on
the ground that the ordinance denied them equal
protection under the Fourteenth Amendment. The
Federal District Court for the Eastern District of
New York upheld the ordinance on the basis that its
goal, the maintenance of the prevailing traditional
family pattern, was appropriately carried out by
zoning regulation. The Circuit Court of Appeals
invalidated the ordinance. It applied the test that
the legislative classification must be reasonable and
bear a rational relationship to the objective sought
to be advanced by the legislation. The court said
first of all that supporting a particular family type
is not a valid zoning objective and, secondly, that
even if it were, the classification is unreasonable. In
other words, whether residents of a dwelling were
related or unrelated had no relationship to the goals
sought to be obtained by the ordinance. For example,
the court said, if Belle Terre wanted to avoid rent in-
flation, it could adopt rent controls; if Belle Terre
wanted to maintain population density at the level
of traditional family units, it could have chosen a
number greater than two unrelated people, because
families are usually greater than two people; if Belle
Terre wanted to avoid excessive automobile traffic
it could limit the number of cars per dwelling. "We
hold," the Circuit Court said, "that since the discriminatory classification is unsupported by any rational basis consistent with permissible zoning law
objectives, it transgresses the Equal Protection
clause."[10] The dissent said that the standard applied
in deciding the case was too strict.

The case was appealed to the Supreme Court. In April 1974, in *Village of Belle Terre* v. *Boraas,* the Court upheld the ordinance, reversing the Court of Appeals. It said that the ordinance bore a reasonable relationship to a permissible state objective—land-use control—and did not involve any deprivation of fundamental rights. The decision is a major setback to collective-living situations.

The Belle Terre ordinance would not have prohibited two unrelated people from living together. On this issue, the Supreme Court said, "It is said that the Belle Terre ordinance reeks with animosity to unmarried couples who live together. . . . There is no evidence to support it; and the provision of the ordinance bringing within the definition of a 'family' two unmarried people belies the charge."[11] But what if the ordinance had prohibited two unrelated people from living together? Would it have been constitutional? Probably not. The Court would first reevaluate whether there was a rational relationship between the classification and the zoning objectives. The Court got that far in evaluating a provision of the Food Stamp Act, which excluded from eligibility any household containing an individual who was unrelated to any other member of the household. In that case, the Court said that the means were not reasonably related to the goals sought to be achieved.[12] If, however, the court affirmed its position in *Belle Terre* v. *Boraas* that the means *were* reasonably related to the ends, it would then have to inquire into whether any fundamental rights were deprived. It would be reasonable for the Court to determine that such an ordinance interferes with the zone of privacy articulated in *Griswold* and extended in *Baird* to unmarried couples. (See pages 40–41.)

Can a Bank Legally Refuse to Let Unmarried People Establish a Joint Bank Account?

No. That would violate the Equal Credit Opportunity Act as discrimination in the granting of credit on the basis of marital status. Most banks are not likely to refuse such an account, because it is usually in a bank's best interest to take the business. However, the problem has arisen where two unmarried people sought to open a joint checking account in a bank that offered free checking privileges. Judith and Martin were told that the privilege was available to related or married people only. Inquiry revealed that the bank officers realized that they were required to offer the same privilege to related and nonrelated customers but that they fostered the policy to keep low the number of people who would take advantage of it. Most people do not get past the bank's refusal and end up taking out a joint account for which they pay service charges.

If You Acquire Real or Personal Property by Gift or Inheritance, to Whom Does It Belong?

Property acquired by gift or inheritance belongs to the person to whom it is given. If Sara's grandmother leaves her a farm, it belongs to Sara; if Eric's friend gives him an umbrella, it belongs to Eric. If someone gave a gift of real or personal property to Eric and Sara, it would be held by them as tenants in common.[13] In community property jurisdictions, a gift or bequest to a married couple is considered community property, so each would get one half its value on dissolution of the marriage.

Who Has the Right to Manage and Control Property Owned by Two Unmarried People Living Together?

Each has the right to manage and control his/her property. Property owned jointly is to be managed jointly. Simple, you say. Why should there be any question? The answer is that you might well be treated differently if you were married.

At least one separate property state, Alabama, provides that a wife may not sell or mortgage her own interest in land unless her husband joins in the deed.[14] The State of Georgia does not permit a woman to agree to assume responsibility for her husband's legal obligations (act as a surety).[15] In Michigan, the husband is given the exclusive right to manage and control property he and his wife hold as tenants by the entirety.[16] The Tennessee Supreme Court decided as recently as 1971 that the husband has the sole right to rents and profits from property held as tenants by the entirety.[17]

Similarly, the married woman in one of the eight community property states—Louisiana—still does not have a right equal to that of her husband to manage and control community property.

Such laws should be challenged as a gender-based discrimination violating the equal-protection clause of the Fourteenth Amendment.

On balance, in those states that retain restrictions on the married woman's ability to contract or manage and control community property, a woman living with a man may be better off than her married counterpart.

Are Unmarried People Who Are Living Together Liable for Each Other's Debts?

No, because liability hinges on the existence of a marriage relationship.

In separate property states, husband and wife are generally not liable for each other's debts. But the husband is liable for debts the wife incurred on his credit for necessaries. Necessaries include food, clothing, shelter, medical and legal services, furniture and other household goods, funeral expenses, and even things that might be considered luxuries to some but that are "necessary" given a certain standard of living.

In community property states, the husband is generally liable for the wife's debts only if they were incurred with his consent. But the wife is liable for his debts in Louisiana, which gives the husband management and control, because he is presumed to be acting on behalf of the marital community. This double standard would cease if the statute giving the husband the exclusive right to manage and control community property were repealed or held unconstitutional.

Can Unmarried People Who Are Living Together Be Required to Support Each Other?

Generally, no. But there may be statutes that require contributions for certain purposes. For example, the New York State Family Court Act, Article 5, Section 514, provides that the father of a child born outside marriage can be required to pay reasonable expenses incurred by the mother in connection with her pregnancy. The law requires an ascertainment of "father-hood" to impose liability. This could be done through an order of filiation or the natural father's acknowl-edgment of paternity. While the statute by no means provides for support, it does establish the pregnant woman's right to reasonable expenses incurred in connection with pregnancy outside of marriage. The court has held "reasonable expenses" to include the cost of a therapeutic abortion,[18] but not the cost of psychotherapy.[19]

In contrast, a husband is required by law to sup-port his wife. She generally has the duty to support him only if he is about to become a public charge. At first glance, this right to support seems like a boon to women. But it has severe inherent drawbacks. The major one is that, basically, the wife has to take what the husband gives her. He does not have to support her at the level he can afford. And a court cannot step in and determine the adequacy of support unless the husband and wife separate. This limitation allows situations to exist such as one in which a wife was left to live in a house with a coal stove and no inside toilet, bathing facilities, or kitchen sink; had no new clothing other than a coat in four years; and got to see one movie in twelve years, even though her hus-band owned assets of close to $300,000 and had a yearly income of $8,000 to $9,000.[20]

Who Gets What When Two People Who Are Living Together Decide to Split Up?

This question was discussed earlier in the chapter, in relation to how people decide to take title to property when they acquire it. The basic rule is that "he who has title gets it." This, we have seen, is in contrast to the way the law treats married people. When married people split up, courts have great discretion in awarding possession of the couple's property. For example, the court can say that it is in the interest of fairness for the wife to get the house even though it is not in her name.

The best way to avoid the trauma of a conflict over who gets what is to agree beforehand. But the rule of thumb to observe is that those agreements, whether oral or written, must be independent of your agreement to live together or have sexual relations.

Will a Court Ever Make Exceptions to the Rule that "He Who Has Title Gets the Property"?

Yes, if you can show that the person with title holds the property for the other's benefit. (See the discussion of resulting trust, page 83.) For example, in a Florida case, Mr. Milligan bought some land on which he and Mrs. Bullington built their house. He fell behind in his payments. She then advanced enough money to cover half the purchase price of the land, but title remained in his name. The court decided that Mr. Milligan held half the property for Mrs. Bullington's benefit because she had paid for it with that understanding.[21] Yet in a Washington case, the court decided differently. Mr. Creasman and Ms. Paul lived together for several years. They bought real estate, in part with Mr. Creasman's money, but they put it in Ms. Paul's name. When Ms. Paul died, Mr. Creasman sued her estate for his interest in the property. But the court said that there was no evidence that Ms. Paul held the property for Mr. Creasman's benefit.[22] So having the property in one person's name is risky. If the property is not in your name, your case would be strongest if you could show that you *lent*, rather than gave, your friend the money to acquire the property.

The other time a court might make an exception is when you are claiming that you were involved in a joint commercial venture. Recently, the Washington court was faced with that problem. Lucy Antoine and Roy Thornton began living together in 1953. At the time, Roy was already married to another woman. Lucy and Roy had four children. In the early fifties, Lucy and Roy began raising cattle. With the profits of the venture, they bought a farm in Roy's name. In 1961, they moved the cattle business to the farm and it prospered. Lucy participated extensively in managing and operating the farm. Roy controlled the finances and held the proceeds in a checking account in his name. When Roy died in 1969, Lucy claimed that she was entitled to half his assets. The court said that to rebut the presumption that Roy owned the property, she would have to prove the existence of a partnership relationship. Her proof that they had both participated equally in the management of the farm was sufficient. But nothing short of that business relationship would do.

In this case, the court put into question its harsh adherence to the presumption that "he who has title gets the property." The court said, "a presumption involving constitutional rights must fall unless there is a substantial assurance that the presumed fact is more likely than not to follow from the proven fact."[23] Here, is the presumed fact—that the titleholder is the owner—more likely than not to follow from the proven fact—namely, that Roy has title? Not in light of other facts, such as the circumstances of purchase, who contributed what and how, the intent of the parties, and so on. The court suggested that the true basis for the "he who has title gets the property" rule is a moral condemnation of "meretricious relationships":

> We are dubious about the continuing validity of this legal presumption or fiction accepted and applied by the court in *Creasman* v. *Boyle*. . . . We have disclaimed, and continue to disclaim, any opinion or intended reflection on the moral status of a couple living in a meretricious relationship. It would appear that the only basis for applying this presumption in the case of a meretricious relationship, and not in the case of an innocent but mistaken belief in the existence of a valid marriage, is that the couple who knows they are not married *must have consciously intended* that the party in whose name title was taken should have the exclusive interest in the property, while the couple who mistakenly thought they were married *must have intended* that each should have the equivalent of a community interest in the property.
>
> Such a thesis or assumption certainly has a moralistic aura, but is realistically and objectively questionable.[24]

Application of the court's thinking could radically change the way assets are distributed. It would require the court to allow the claimant to adduce proof of his/her interest when faced with a situation where one person holds title and the other claims an interest. This is permitted now, certainly, but the burden of proof would be less because there would no longer be a presumption that in a "meretricious relationship" the titleholder was intended to be the owner.

Will a Community Property State Apply Community Property Principles to Unmarried People Living Together?

No. The right to one half the assets of a marriage depends on the existence of a valid marriage or the good-faith belief that there was one. Of course, if you can demonstrate that you carried on a business together, as in *Thornton*, that is another story. But even there, the assets you split up are only those derived from the business relationship, nothing else. One recent California case looks like an exception but is really not.

Paul Cary and Janet Forbes lived together in California for eight years. They knew they were not married and talked of having a wedding but never got around to it. They had four children, whom Paul acknowledged and supported. Janet used the name "Cary" and took care of the house and children while Paul worked outside the home. They represented themselves to others as husband and wife. In 1971, Paul sought to have the "marriage" annulled, despite the fact that California does not recognize common-law marriage (in effect, there was no marriage). Janet claimed one half the property acquired during the eight years. The court allowed her to do so. At first glance, it looks as if the California court eliminated the distinction between marriage and living together. But that is emphatically not so. The court placed great emphasis on the existence of a "family" relationship and specifically said that its rule did not apply to casual living-together arrangements. The court said:

> It should be pointed out that the criterion for application of the rule we apply to the case before us is much more than that of an unmarried living arrangement between a man and a woman. The Family Law Act obviously requires that there be established not only an ostensible marital relationship but also an actual family relationship, with cohabitation and mutual recognition and assumption of the usual rights, duties and obligations attending marriage.[25]

So California would not apply community property principles to unmarried people living together unless they constituted a "family."

Is There Any Advantage to Being Married as Far as the Laws of Inheritance Are Concerned?

Yes. If a person dies without a will, his/her estate (what he/she owned at death) is distributed according to a statutory scheme that favors the spouse, the children, and other relatives, in that order. For example, in New York, if a husband dies without a will and leaves a wife, she takes all.[26] If he dies leaving a wife and one child, each takes one half. If he dies leaving a wife and more than one child, she takes one third and the children divide the remainder equally. In contrast, if you are not married and die without a will, your property will go to your blood relatives, not to the person you are living with.

There is another way in which marriage remains a plus. That is in something called the "right of election," or the "elective share." That means that when a spouse dies, no matter what his/her will provides, the surviving spouse may "elect," or choose to take, a portion of the estate. The portion is set by statute and varies according to whether or not there are children as well.[27] The purpose of the law is to prevent one spouse from disinheriting the other. The only way you can disinherit a spouse is by giving all your property away long before you die. If you are unmarried and living together, neither of you is entitled to an elective share.

A third area in which inheritance laws favor married couples is in estate taxes. In a community property state, since each spouse owns one half of the assets, only one half passes through the estate of the one who dies and is taxed. In a separate property state, all the property to which a person has title passes through his/her estate and is taxed. To remedy this inequity, Congress amended the Internal Revenue Code to provide for a "marital deduction." Here is how it works: In the separate property states, either one half of the gross estate or the value of the property left to the surviving spouse, whichever is *less*, is tax-exempt. If the whole estate is left to the surviving spouse, one half is tax-exempt, just as in the community property states. For example, a wife has a house worth $40,000 in her name and nothing else. When she dies, she leaves the house to her husband. One half of the gross estate is $20,000; the value of the property left to the surviving spouse is $40,000. The marital deduction is the lesser of the two: $20,000. But suppose the wife has a house worth $40,000 and a bank account of $10,000. When she dies, she leaves the house to her husband and the bank account to her daughter. One half of the gross estate is $25,000; the value of the property left to the surviving spouse is $40,000. The marital deduction is the lesser of the two: $25,000. If you are unmarried and living together, you cannot take advantage of the marital deduction.

What Can People Who Are Unmarried and Living Together Do to Ensure that Each Will Inherit the Other's Property on Death?

The best method is to make a valid will. To be valid in New York, a will must be in writing, signed by the maker, and witnessed by at least two people who are not beneficiaries of the will. Other states require three witnesses. Remember that if you own land, you must meet the requirements for a valid will in the state where the land is located. The only problem that could arise is that if one of you is married to someone else, the spouse could claim his/her elective share. So if you are living with someone who is already married, he/she should obtain a divorce.

Short of a will, holding property jointly or in trust may effect your purposes. But again, joint tenancies and trusts are not immune to a spouse's right of election.

Do Unmarried People Living Together Have the Right to Sue for Each Other's Wrongful Death?

No. Suppose one of you gets hit by a car and dies. The dead person's "distributees" have the right to sue for his/her wrongful death. "Distributees" are the same people who inherit if you die without a will—the spouse, children, and relatives. Note that the right to sue for wrongful death cannot be conveyed even by means of a will. That is because the right to sue belongs to the distributees, not to the deceased's estate.

Do Unmarried People Who Are Living Together Have the Right to Sue for Injury Either One Suffered before Death?

No. Suppose one of you gets a broken leg when the stairs in your apartment building cave in. Then, a few months later, the same person dies of a heart attack. He/she had the right to sue the landlord but died before he/she could do so. This right to sue is known as a survival action because it survives death. The right to sue vests in the deceased's personal estate. Because it does so, it may be conveyed by will.[28] If there were no will, the proceeds of such a suit would go to the distributees. But if there is a will, the beneficiaries will be entitled to the proceeds.

Do Unmarried People Who Are Living Together Have the Right to Sue for Loss of Consortium?

No. Consortium is the legal right of one spouse to the comfort, affection, services, and society of the other. It also includes support and sexual relations. The ability to maintain an action for loss of consortium depends on the existence of a valid marriage.

NOTES

1. Louisiana Statutes Annotated, C.C. Art. 2404 (West 1971).

2. Arizona Revised Statutes, § 25–214 (West 1973); California Annotated Civil Code, § 5125 (West 1976 Supp); General Laws of Idaho Annotated, § 32–912 (1975 Supp); New Mexico Statutes Annotated, § 57–4A–8 (1975 Supp); Nevada Revised Statutes, Chap. 123.230 (1975); Vernon's Texas Family Code Annotated, § 5.22 (West 1975 Supp); Revised Code of Washington Annotated, § 26.16.030 (West 1975 Supp).

3. N.Y.S. Domestic Relations Law, § 234 (McKinney's 1964).

4. N.Y.S. Estates Powers and Trust Law, § 5–1.1 (McKinney's 1964).

5. Gini Kopecky, "Housing: Getting Your Foot in the Door," *Ms.* May 1975, pp. 103–106.

6. N.Y.C. Administrative Code § B1–7.0, 5(a) (!)–(2).

7. 15 U.S.C. §§ 1691 et seq., effective October 28, 1975.

8. Colorado, Florida, Illinois, Maryland, Massachusetts, Minnesota, New Jersey, New York, Oregon, Rhode Island, Vermont, Washington, Wisconsin. See Margaret Gates, "Credit Discrimination against Women: Causes and Solutions," *Vanderbilt Law Review* 27 (April 1974), pp. 409, 436.

9. *Edwards* v. *Roe*, 327 N.Y.S.2d 307, 309, 68 Misc. 2d 278 (1971).

10. *Boraas* v. *Belle Terre*, 476 F.2d 806, 808 (E.D.N.Y. 1973).

11. *Village of Belle Terre* v. *Boraas*, 416 U.S. 1, 8 (1974).

12. *U.S. Department of Agriculture* v. *Moreno*, 413 U.S. 528 (1973).

13. Under a new provision of the N.Y.S. Estates Powers and Trusts Law (§ 6–2.2), a disposition of real property to an unmarried couple creates in them a joint tenancy, but only if they are described in it as husband and wife.

14. Code of Alabama, Title 34, § 73 (1959).

15. Georgia Code Annotated, § 53–503 (1974).

16. Michigan Compiled Laws Annotated, § 557.101 (West 1967).

17. *Weaks* v. *Gress,* S. Ct. Tenn., 474 S.W.2d 424 (1971).

18. *Gladys C.* v. *Robert L.,* 305 N.Y.S.2d 69, 61 Misc. 2d 381 (1969).

19. *Anonymous* v. *Anonymous,* 265 N.Y.S.2d 827, 48 Misc. 2d 794 (1965).

20. *McGuire* v. *McGuire,* 157 Neb. 226, 59 N.W.2d 336 (1953).

21. *Williams* v. *Bullington,* S. Ct. Fla., 32 So. 2d 273 (1947).

22. *Creasman* v. *Boyle,* S. Ct. Wash., 196 P.2d 835 (1948).

23. *Antoine* v. *Thornton,* 81 Wash. 2d 72, 499 P.2d 864, 866 (1972). The term "meretricious" appears frequently in cases involving unmarried couples. It means here "of or relating to a prostitute; having a harlot's traits" (Webster's Third International Dictionary).

24. *Ibid.,* pp. 866–867.

25. *In re Marriage of Cary,* 34 Cal. App. 3d 345, 109 Cal. Rptr. 862 (1973).

26. N.Y.S. Estates Powers and Trusts Law, § 4–1.1 (McKinney's 1964).

27. *Ibid.,* § 5–1.1.

28. *Ibid.,* § 11–3.2–.3.

6 / Contracts

The chapter on property raises two kinds of problems
unmarried people living together may face: those
involving their relations with the community and
those involving their relations with each other. The
problems in the first category can be resolved only
through a combination of education and legal action.
Can the problems of the second category be resolved
by contract between the parties? Before exploring
this possibility in more detail, some background will
be useful.

What Is a Contract?

A contract is a promise to do something in exchange
for someone else's promise to do something. This just
means it is an agreement or a bargain between
parties. Some contracts are required to be in writing
—for instance, a contract to buy or sell real estate,
a contract in consideration of marriage, or a contract
to bequeath property or establish a trust.[1]

Is Marriage a Contract?

Marriage is often spoken of as a contract. But in actuality, the only agreement the parties make is the decision to get married. From then on, the state law is the third party to the marriage and governs their relationship. Marriage is, in fact, a legally defined status, not a contract.

Are Married People Legally Capable of Making Contracts with Each Other?

Yes, although this has not always been so. Historically, the husband and wife were viewed as one person; therefore, it was thought that there could be no contract between them because there weren't two parties. The Married Women's Property Acts enacted in the United States in the mid-nineteenth century accorded a married woman the right to contract, including the right to contract with her spouse. But even today, a state may impose limits on a married couple's ability to contract. For example, New York State General Obligations Law, Section 5–311, says that they may not contract to dissolve the marriage (they must get a divorce) or to waive the wife's right to support. The latter provision extends even beyond marriage. A woman cannot contract away her right to alimony. If she does, it may be reinstituted by a court.

Are Unmarried People Capable of Making Contracts with Each Other?

Unmarried people have never suffered such disability to contract. In fact, it has been common for centuries for unmarried people to make antenuptial contracts in consideration of marriage.

What Restrictions Have Courts Placed on Contracts between Married People?

The courts will enforce contracts regarding property made between married people as long as (1) they don't concern the obligation of the husband to provide support and the obligation of the wife to provide sexual, housekeeping, and child-rearing services; and (2) they are not contracts in contemplation of divorce. For example, Mr. and Mrs. Garlock made a contract under which he was to pay her $15,000 per year for her natural life in equal monthly installments in fulfillment of his obligation to support her. Mr. Garlock failed to pay certain installments. Mrs. Garlock sued. But the court held their agreement to be void and denied her the payments. The court was afraid that a wife might be induced to sign a contract where she would be given less than her husband could afford.[2] The usual reasons for not enforcing agreements to change the support/services obligations are that such agreements would promote marital controversy, be subject to undue influence, and lack something that is exchanged—you can't promise to do what you are already legally bound to do.

The courts will not enforce contracts in contemplation of divorce for similar reasons: they tend to encourage divorce, they may be subject to undue influence, they might be inflexible in the face of changed circumstances of the parties.

What Challenges Can Be Made to the Courts' Reluctance to Enforce Contracts within Marriage?

Perhaps the argument could be made that the support/services obligations are sex discriminatory in violation of the equal-protection clause. It is unreasonable to tie duties within a marriage to gender. Men who wish to do housework and women who wish to work outside the home are discriminated against. So contracts modifying these obligations should be within the capacity of the husband and wife.

The reluctance to enforce contracts in contemplation of divorce could perhaps be combatted by showing that such contracts do not encourage divorce but merely clarify matters between the spouses. Also, as state divorce laws are relaxed, such agreements cannot be said to promote collusive divorce, since collusion is unnecessary. Instead, they will facilitate property settlements. Finally, undue influence and flexibility can be dealt with via general principles of contract law.[3]

What Kinds of Problems Might Unmarried People Living Together Wish to Resolve by Contract?

They may wish to resolve for themselves exactly those problems state law resolves (sometimes unsatisfactorily) for married people: (1) who owns what property and who manages it, (2) who gets what in the event of a separation, (3) who supports whom in exchange for what. In addition, there may be myriad non-property-related problems—such as where they live, children, responsibility for birth control, mutual household obligations, and the like—that they would like to resolve by agreement. The psychological value of these agreements may be great in that they require the couple to communicate and eliminate potential sources of conflict. But the law has not yet reached the point where it will enforce such agreements. Because the chances of enforcing property contracts are much greater, these are the ones we will be concerned with.

Will the Courts Enforce Contracts concerning Property between Unmarried People Living Together?

Yes, and there is perhaps more latitude to contract effectively between unmarried than between married people because the courts cannot view your contract as a subversion of the institution of marriage.

The basic problem is that these contracts must be independent of your agreement to cohabit or to have sexual relations.

What Kinds of Agreements Will Stand Up in Court?

First, let us look at the kind of agreement that will *not* stand up in court. A choice example is the agreement that was at issue in an 1898 New York case. There, a man and a woman agreed to live together "for mutual love and affection" and agreed that their earnings would be held jointly and used for their joint benefit and support during their lives. To anyone today who is not disturbed by the "immorality" of their relationship, this seems like a perfectly reasonable, even admirable and egalitarian, agreement. But to the court then, and probably now, the agreement was anathema. The court held that since the agreement to pool earnings was not separate from the agreement to cohabit, it was illegal and could not be enforced.[4] Where cohabitation or fornication is what you are giving for what you are getting in exchange, the agreement will not be upheld.

Paradoxically, that is true even in states that do not consider fornication or cohabitation illegal. It is possible that the courts don't uphold these kinds of agreements because they look too much like prostitution. Another explanation could be that such agreements tend to subvert the formal marriage relationship. If people can provide for their economic needs through a contract, why should they involve the state by getting formally married?

The courts will, however, uphold agreements made between unmarried cohabitors if the quid pro quo has nothing to do with their illicit relationship. For example, a man and a woman who lived together agreed that each of them would contribute to the purchase price and maintenance of some real estate and each would have an equal share of the property.

The court said that although it did not condone the relationship, the agreement was legal and upheld the equal division.[5]

In a more recent case, the Michigan Court of Appeals decided that a woman, Mrs. Tyranski, was entitled to a house that was in the name of the man she had been living with, Mr. Lattavo. Mrs. Tyranski was a waitress; Mr. Lattavo was a truck driver. At the time they met, they were each married to other people. They began living together in about 1963. Four years later, they had a house built that they lived in until Mr. Lattavo died in 1969. Mrs. Tyranski sued his estate for the house. The judge decided that Mrs. Tyranski and Mr. Lattavo had made an oral agreement that the house would be hers if she contributed $10,000 toward its construction and if she did the housekeeping, cooking, laundry, and entertaining. The evidence showed that Mrs. Tyranski had done all these things and that she had "changed the tenor of her life" in performance of the agreement. The court, quoting a U.S. Supreme Court case, said "equity does not demand that its suitors shall have led blameless lives." The judge held that there was nothing illegal about their agreement and the nature of their relationship was irrelevant. Even though cohabitation is a crime in Michigan, the agreement was upheld. The judge wrote: "Mrs. Tyranski was able to establish the contract to transfer the Blue Skies house to her without reference to her sexual relationship with Mr. Lattavo." He then wrote: "Where a meretricious relationship has already been entered upon, to penalize one of the parties by striking down their otherwise lawful promises, will not undo the relationship, nor is it likely to discourage others from entering upon such relationships."[6] This is one of the most recent and most enlightened opinions on the subject. It will provide valuable ammunition in the struggle to gain judicial recognition of agreements made between people who are living together.

What Challenges Can Be Made to the Courts' Reluctance to Enforce Contracts between Unmarried People Living Together?

The first is that in those states where cohabitation is not illegal, the courts should be persuaded that there are no rational grounds for considering contracts made between people who are living together illegal. In those states where cohabitation is illegal, efforts should be made to invalidate those laws on the ground that the state has no interest in regulating noncommercial sexual relations between consenting adults and such regulation violates their right to privacy as established in *Eisenstadt* v. *Baird* (see page 41), and furthermore, that their living situation is irrelevant to the validity of their agreements.

NOTES

1. See N.Y.S. General Obligations Law, § 5–701 (McKinney's 1964).
2. *Garlock* v. *Garlock,* 279 N.Y. 337, 255 A.D. 752, 18 N.E.2d 521 (1939).
3. For a detailed discussion of this subject, see Lenore Weitzman, "Legal Regulation of Marriage: Tradition

and Change," *California Law Review* 62 (1974), pp. 1169, 1263–1269.

4. *Vincent* v. *Moriarty,* 52 N.Y.S. 579, 31 A.D. 484 (1898).

5. *Muller* v. *Sobol,* 97 N.Y.S.2d 905, 277 A.D. 884, rehearing and leave to appeal denied 99 N.Y.S.2d 757 (1950).

6. *Tyranski* v. *Piggins,* 44 Mich. App. 570, 205 N.W.2d 595, 598 (1973).

7 / Living Together and Divorce

You are divorced. You have custody of your children and are receiving alimony. You meet a man or woman you like a lot. The painful memories of your marriage and divorce are still clear in your mind. You do not wish to make the same mistakes again. You wish to be more cautious, more knowledgeable, this time around. You would like to get to know each other better and you feel the best way is by living together.

What effect does the fact that you are living with someone have on your right to alimony and the custody of your children?

Can Your Alimony Be Cut Off Because You Are Living with Someone?

Yes. The state laws governing alimony uniformly provide the courts with broad discretionary powers to alter the award of alimony because of changed circumstances of the parties. Some states allow either the husband or the wife to receive alimony. More commonly, the wife alone is eligible. The right to alimony is based on her right to support during the marriage. If a judge takes the view that the presence of a new man in the house means that she has a new source of support, he/she may decide that this constitutes a change in circumstances. He/she may decide that this change in circumstances is so substantial as to warrant a reduction or elimination of the alimony award, even though the person you are living with may in fact give you no support and even though he has no legal obligations to do so.

New York is the one state, to my knowledge, that *expressly* permits judges to do this. Section 248 of the Domestic Relations Law says:

> The court in its discretion upon application of the husband on notice, upon proof that the wife is habitually living with another man and holding herself out as his wife, although not married to such man, may modify such final judgment and any orders made with respect thereto by annulling the provisions of such final judgment or orders or of both, directing payment of money for the support of such wife.

Although in theory living together could jeopardize your right to alimony, in practice the courts have been reluctant to let that happen. New York's statute has not yet been successfully used to deprive a woman of alimony, although several ex-husbands have tried to do so.

Elsa and Edwin Rosenberg were married in 1954 and had two children. They separated in 1959. Their separation agreement stated that she would receive $30 a week support until her remarriage. They were divorced in 1960 and the terms of the separation agreement were incorporated in the divorce decree. In 1961, Edwin stopped paying; in 1963, Elsa sued. Edwin argued that he should not have to pay her alimony because she was living with a man who was contributing toward the expense of maintaining the household. The court decided that Edwin had to keep paying. Why? Because their agreement said that she would be entitled to alimony "until her remarriage." Since she hadn't remarried, she was still entitled to payment. The court said Section 248 did not apply to separation agreements, but only to final judgments of divorce or annulment.[1] This is a bit of weasling, because the separation agreement is a mere substitute for the alimony provisions in a final judgment—if there had been no separation agreement and the same alimony had been provided for by the final judgment of divorce, Section 248 would have applied.

The same result was reached in Brooklyn in 1974. Thomas Josephs sued for divorce on grounds of cruel and inhuman treatment. According to the court, his wife was "a confirmed alcoholic, a woman of loose morals who has frittered away her life on liquor and immorality with no comprehension of her responsibilities and obligations to her husband and family."[2] Even though he did not have to, Thomas agreed to support her after the divorce. A stipulation to this effect was incorporated in the final judgment of divorce. It said he would pay her $150 a week during her life or until her remarriage. When Judith began living with a man, Thomas went to court to have the alimony reduced or eliminated under Section 248. The court denied his request. Why? Because the stipulation did not provide for termination on proof of her "immorality."

What do these cases tell us? If you are a man, make sure your separation agreement says you will pay alimony only until the death of either you or your wife, until her remarriage, or until she begins living with a man. If you are a woman, you should try to keep this provision out. The clause that would be fairest to both men and women is one that provides for the payment of alimony until the recipient receives support from another source. Alimony should be based on need. When the need ceases, so should the alimony. If a woman lives with a man, it does not necessarily mean that he supports her.

In other states, men whose former wives are living with another man have sought to have their alimony obligations terminated by arguing that the wife's living with a man constitutes a change in circumstances warranting the court's intervention. So far, the argument has not persuaded any higher courts.

In Florida, a Mr. and Ms. Sheffield were divorced in 1968; their decree said he would pay her $600 a month until her remarriage. In 1969, she began living with Mr. Schoenfield. The court said since in Florida adultery was not an automatic bar to alimony, fornication could not be the basis for terminating it. The court also said:

> It is obvious that a ceremonial marriage offers various benefits, as well as legal rights, duties and obligations which do not obtain in the wife's relationship with Mr. Schoenfield. He is under no obligation to support her, or even to stay with her, and she is neither entitled to dower or government social security benefits upon his death, nor is she recognized by the world at large as Schoenfield's wife.[3]

The Arkansas Supreme Court has also held that if the separation agreement provided for termination of alimony upon remarriage, it meant *remarriage,* not living together. It also decided that it did not have the power to prohibit the ex-wife from living with a man.[4]

An Illinois court has decided that while living

together is not grounds for terminating alimony, it is grounds for modifying it downward. Pursuant to the divorce decree, Mrs. Hall got a $100,000 house, $9,600 a year, a car, and some insurance policies. The man living with her, Mr. Jones, made $11,500 a year and, aside from occasional purchases of groceries and gasoline, made no financial contribution to the maintenance of the household. The court decided that a downward modification would be proper, since it was unfair for Dr. Hall to be paying for Mr. Jones's upkeep.[5]

Does Your Child of a Prior Marriage Have Any Rights vis-à-vis the Person You Live With?

The child does not have the right to be supported by the person you live with unless adoption has occurred or unless you marry each other; that much is clear.

The harder question is, Does the child who lives with you have any legal say in whether your roommate stays or goes? Probably not. Just about the only thing the child can do is complain to the noncustodial parent, who could then sue for a change in custody.

Can You Be Deprived of Custody of Your Children of a Prior Marriage Because You Are Living with Someone?

Suppose Peter and Judith were married and had a child. On divorce, the court awarded Judith custody of the child. Judith began living with Martin. Peter goes back to court and seeks custody of the child on the ground that Judith is unfit. What will the court do?

The answer hinges on whether the particular judge considers living with someone out of wedlock to be a sign of unfitness. That depends on the judge's attitudes toward sex and his/her perception of the attitudes held by the community.

The problem has not been dealt with in all states. However, some state courts have spoken.

A New York State court ruled that although the mother of a six-year-old boy was living with a man, her life-style did not render her unfit to keep custody of the child. The judge was quoted as saying that she could hardly be designated for a "mother of the year award" but that "residence together of an unmarried male and female without benefit of a sermonized marriage is not per se evil or immoral."[6]

The New Hampshire Supreme Court similarly decided that the fact that a woman was keeping company in her home with an unmarried man shortly after her separation from her husband was insufficient to deprive her of custody.[7]

The North Carolina Court of Appeals held that there was insufficient evidence to show that a child had been adversely affected by his new stepfather's "premarital visits" with his mother, and therefore his mother could not be deprived of custody.[8]

In Minnesota, a father who was living with his girlfriend was permitted to retain custody of his two sons, whom he had had for seven years. The court said that the fact he was living with a woman was not such a substantial change in circumstances as to warrant a change of custody. Instead, the judge concentrated on what would be in the best interests

of the children, considering the psychological need
for continuity in the relationship. The court said
about the man and his friend, "Some marriages are
not stable environments in which to raise children,
and some informal relationships are very stable and
can provide the emotional, psychological and physical security necessary to raising children." It added
further on, "With an increasing number of marriage
dissolutions and many remarriages, one must certainly question the relative morality of multiple
marriages as opposed to informal living arrangements."[9] This is a most enlightened opinion. It
concentrates on the child's concerns rather than
making moral judgments or presuming that living
together is tantamount to parental unfitness.

Courts in Oklahoma, Georgia, Florida, Louisiana,
and Nevada have taken the position that women
can be deprived of custody not only for living with
a man, but also for having sexual relations. Of these
states, cohabitation is illegal only in Florida and
fornication is illegal in Florida and Georgia.

The Nevada Supreme Court switched custody
of four children from the mother, who was "keeping
company with a man late at night and into the
morning," to the father. The judge said, "The intimate relationship of appellant [the mother] and
her paramour in close proximity of children of
tender years may be deemed a harmful influence upon
those children by a trial court."[10] However, under
a prior decision, a mother was permitted to retain
custody, since the custody award was made to her
while she was living with a man, not *before* she
adopted her "evil" ways.

The Oklahoma Court of Appeals changed custody
from mother to father because the mother slept

with another man several nights a week. The court dubbed this situation a "countercultural environment" and assumed, without proof, that it would harm the child.[11] The Supreme Court of Georgia affirmed a change in custody from mother to father on the basis that she refused to testify against the man she was living with. Rejecting Fifth Amendment arguments, the court said an unfavorable inference of illicit conduct could be drawn from her refusal to testify.[12] A Florida District Court of Appeals changed custody of a three-year-old from mother to father because the woman had intercourse with a man to whom she was not married while separated from her husband and while the child was also at home. The court said, "A female parent who commits adultery in the presence of her child can hardly be called a 'mother' in the traditional American sense."[13] The same judge held that a mother who admitted having sexual relations in her home was unfit to have custody.[14]

Interestingly enough, while all this was done in the name of the best interests of the child, there was no evidence that the children were in fact adversely affected by their mothers' behavior. In addition, while these may not be all the cases on the subject, all of them involve depriving women of custody because of their sexual activity. Would the judge look upon men in the same way? This may be another area in which a double standard is applied.

NOTES

1. *Rosenberg* v. *Rosenberg*, 260 N.Y.S.2d 508, 512, 46 Misc. 2d 693 (1965).

2. *Josephs* v. *Josephs*, 358 N.Y.S.2d 326, 329, 78 Misc. 2d 723 (1974).

3. *Sheffield* v. *Sheffield*, Fla. App., 310 So. 2d 410 (1975).

4. *Sturgis* v. *Sturgis*, 1 Family Law Reporter 2042 (Ark. Sup. Ct., October 19, 1974).

5. *Hall* v. *Hall*, 25 Ill. App. 3d 524, 323 N.E.2d 541 (1975).

6. *New York Times*, April 26, 1975.

7. *Del Pozzo* v. *Del Pozzo*, S. Ct. N.H., 309 A.2d 151 (1973).

8. *Blackley* v. *Blackley*, 18 N.C. App. 535, 197 S.E.2d 243 (1973).

9. *Torrance* v. *Torrance*, 1 Family Law Reporter 2456 (Minn. April 3, 1975).

10. *Culbertson* v. *Culbertson*, S. Ct. Nev., 533 P.2d 768 (1975).

11. *Brim* v. *Brim*, Okla. App., 532 P.2d 1403 (1975).

12. *Simpson* v. *Simpson*, 233 Ga. 17, 209 S.E.2d 611 (1974).

13. *Dinkel* v. *Dinkel*, Fla. App., 305 So. 2d 90 (1974).

14. *Young* v. *Young*, Fla. App., 305 So. 2d 92 (1974).

8 / Employment

The fact that you are living with someone is not exactly the kind of thing you put on your résumé. But sooner or later, someone at your job is going to find out about your living situation. If you live in a small community, it's unavoidable. If you are not ashamed of your living situation, you'll probably be open about it anyway. What are the consequences?

At this moment, a case is pending appeal in which a woman was fired from her position as a schoolteacher in a small community because she was living with a man. Depending upon what you do for a living, or the attitudes of the community in which you live, you may be risking your jobs by living together. The legality of firing a person for living with another is uncertain. Employers have very few restrictions on their right to hire or fire. There are statutes that prohibit discrimination in hiring and firing on the basis of sex, national origin, race, religion, or age, but there are none that give you protection for living together. If you are fired because you are living together, your only recourse is to sue your employer for violation of your constitutional rights. Convincing a judge that your rights have been violated will be even more complicated if cohabitation is a crime in the state in which you live.

On the other side of the coin is, Well, would I be

better off married? Oddly enough, marriage too can be a liability as far as employment is concerned.

Employers look for people who will become married to their jobs. Women who are already married to *men* will no doubt have divided loyalty—not to mention less time and energy for the job. It was not until the early 1970's that you had your first chance to meet a married stewardess. In addition, to this day, nepotism rules prohibiting simultaneous employment of husband and wife persist in many businesses. Even when there is the choice of who leaves, it is the woman who is usually sacrificed because she tends to earn less money.

Title VII of the 1964 Civil Rights Act prohibits discrimination in employment. But it does not cover discrimination based on marital status or living situation. To fall within the protection of the law you must show that you have been discriminated against because of your sex (or race, religion, national origin, or age). This brought about the end of the airlines' no-marriage policy because it was directed solely against women. But it cannot always be used to resolve the nepotism problem.

Employment is one area of life in which our constitutional rights to privacy and due process are affected over and over again. How much does an employer have the right to know about you? Is your marital status or the company you keep or your sexual behavior relevant to your job capabilities? Is an employer entitled to make the double-standard judgment that a man becomes a better job risk while a woman becomes a worse one by virtue of marriage? Where "morality" is a criterion for the job, whose standard of morality should prevail—yours? the employer's? the community's? The answers to these questions are only beginning to be explored.

Can You Be Denied a Job or Dismissed for Living with Someone?

Yes. Unfortunately this has occurred, and it is now being contested in the courts. A private employer may hire or fire you at will as long as he, she, or it does not violate the Title VII prohibitions against discrimination on the basis of race, religion, national origin, age, or sex. If your moral code deviates from that of your employer, it is his, her, or its prerogative to fire or not to hire you.

The situation is different for employment in the public sector. Public employers—like police departments, school boards, post offices—are subject to the principles enunciated in the Fourteenth Amendment: no state shall make a law denying any person within its jurisdiction equal protection of the law. For this reason, the challenges to dismissals from employment for living together have arisen in the public sector.

Kathleen Sullivan was dismissed from her job as an elementary school teacher in a small South Dakota town for "gross immorality"—she was living with a man without benefit of marriage. Two out of seven families with children in her class complained to the school board and submitted a petition for her ouster signed by 140 persons in the area. Kathleen appealed her dismissal in the Federal District Court for South Dakota on the grounds that she was denied her constitutional rights to due process, privacy, and freedom of association. The

judge, however, upheld her dismissal. He said that
in order for the school board to dismiss a teacher
"there must be a nexus between the conduct to be
proscribed and the workings of the educational system." He concluded that there was such a nexus
by the following analysis:

> Here, the board found that the teacher's conduct was
> an affront to the moral standards of the community,
> and that its continuance set a bad example for the
> young impressionable students. This court cannot
> say that the reasons for discharge were unrelated to
> the educational process. The board was reasonable
> in its belief that the teacher's personal conduct would
> have an adverse effect upon the pupils she was teach-
> ing. In the hearing before the board, a strong com-
> munity reaction to the teacher's conduct was shown.
> It is reasonable to conclude that the controversy
> between the teacher and the community would make
> it difficult for her to maintain the proper educational
> setting in her classroom.[1]

The decision can be questioned on several
grounds. First, the court did not really demonstrate
a "nexus between the conduct to be proscribed and
the workings of the educational system." It merely
made assumptions that the children would be adversely affected but did not identify what that adverse
effect was nor demonstrate that it had occurred. The
court seemed to be saying that teaching would be
impossible because of the community's reaction. But
then it would be the community's behavior, not the
teacher's conduct, that would disrupt the educational
system. The real analysis the court should have made
was what effect did Kathleen's living with her friend
have on her ability to teach.

Second, the court never acknowledged that this

case presented an invasion of privacy issue. Yet private sexual activity has been recognized as protected by the Ninth Amendment in *Griswold* v. *Connecticut* and *Eisenstadt* v. *Baird*. (See pages 40–41.) Where an important constitutional right is at stake, merely showing a reasonable governmental interest is not enough. You must show a governmental interest so substantial as to justify deprivation of the right. We may question whether governmental concern with the "morality" of the individual or with the reaction of the community to his/her conduct is sufficient.

Third, even if one could show such a substantial governmental interest, it might be more appropriately vindicated through imposition of criminal penalties on cohabitation (which themselves may present constitutional problems) than by conditioning receipt of a governmental benefit—employment by a school district—on the giving up of the constitutional right to privacy.

There may also have been an issue of sex discrimination in this case. Was it a coincidence that the person dismissed was a woman? Were there male teachers living with women who were permitted to remain employed? Perhaps the facts in this case did not warrant a charge of sex discrimination; however, it should be kept in mind in litigation of this sort.

The *Sullivan* decision is distressing because it is "persuasive"—other courts may follow it when faced with the same or similar problems. The legality of dismissal for living together is tenuous in view of the constitutionally protected right to privacy. But you will be living with ambiguity until the higher courts have spoken on this question.

Kathleen Sullivan's case was not the first to raise the question whether a person can be dismissed for living with someone. In 1967, Neil Mindel, a post office clerk in California, was informed that he did not meet the "suitability requirements" for employment in the federal service because his living with a woman he was not married to constituted "immoral conduct." He was dismissed from his job and appealed. The Federal District Court for the Northern District of California (the same level court as decided the *Sullivan* case) decided that Neil's dismissal was unconstitutional for two reasons. First, the post office had failed to show that Neil's private sex life had any connection with the responsibilities of his position; therefore his dismissal was arbitrary and a denial of due process. Second, the post office had failed to show a "compelling reason" as required by *Griswold* to justify invasion of Neil's Ninth Amendment right to privacy.[2]

The *Sullivan* court did not mention the *Mindel* case, although it would seem that it was pertinent.

When a person is dismissed from his/her job for living with someone and this can be shown to constitute sex discrimination, the dismissal is illegal. Ms. X was a switchboard operator. She was dismissed from her job for having an affair and living with Mr. Y, an employee of the same company. He testified that he went to her work area more than she went to his and that his work performance was more adversely affected than hers by their association. But he was merely reprimanded, not fired. Ms. X brought her case to the Equal Employment Opportunity Commission (EEOC), charging discrimination based on sex in violation of Title VII of the 1964 Civil Rights Act. The Commission found sex discrimination. It said, "The evidence supports the conclusion that at least part of the reason why the charging party [Ms. X] was disciplined more severely than the male was that [she] was a female."[3] That does not mean that you cannot be dismissed for living together. It does mean that if one of you is dismissed, the other must go too or the employer is subject to the charge of sex discrimination.

One caveat: If you are confronted by your employer with the fact that you are living with someone, you may be tempted to deny it. Of course there are factual variations—if he stays at your house occasionally, you are not really "living together," and so on. But if it is true, it is wise to tell the truth. If you are then fired, your recourse is a complaint of sex discrimination with the EEOC or an appeal in court on constitutional grounds. If you deny that you are living together and the truth later comes to light, your denial may stand in the way of your reinstatement. That is what happened to Frederick Williams. He was employed as a criminal investigator for the Internal Revenue Service. They confronted him with the fact that he was living with a woman. He wrote an affidavit saying she was married to another man who was also living in the house. It turned out that the other man was her brother, not her husband. The IRS fired Fred for making false statements and the court upheld his dismissal. The concurring opinion said that even though the IRS's inquiry into Fred's private life may have been improper, he did not have the right to answer untruthfully.[4]

Can You Be Denied a Job Because You Are Married?

Yes, as long as the employer's nonmarriage policy is applied to both men and women. But there's the hitch. Have you ever seen an ad saying, "No married men need apply"? It is primarily married women who have been the victims of no-marriage policies.

Employers have not liked married women as employees for several reasons. For one, they don't project the image of sexual availability that attracts customers. For another, they are thought to lack the stability and primary loyalty to job that employers seek. She'll leave when she gets pregnant, she can't travel because then who will cook and clean, she'll stay home when her husband or children get sick, and so on.

However, although married women still face job discrimination in practice, in theory they cannot be discriminated against. The litigation in this area has focused on the airlines' practice of firing flight attendants when they got married and hiring them only if they were unmarried. Male attendants faced no such restrictions on their marital status. Among other things, the airlines said that their customers preferred single flight attendants. But the courts weren't convinced. They said that the fact that the no-marriage policy was applied to women but not to men made it discriminatory and it had to go.[5]

Sex discrimination also arises where marriage is thought to get in the way of job performance. For example, Mrs. A was not allowed a position on a traveling sales force because her husband had been ill for several years and the employer wanted someone "without family considerations" that would prevent travel. The employer did not state that it would reject a male whose wife had been ill. The EEOC said that the employer's policy was based upon a stereotyped view of the family responsibilities of females and that it discriminated because of sex.[6]

What all this means is that if you think you are being discriminated against because you are married, look hard for sex discrimination. But if the boss of Swingin' Singles, Inc. says, "No marrieds need apply," there is little you can do besides drag him into court on grounds of interference with the right to marry.

Can You Be Denied a Job or Fired Because You Are Single?

Sure, except if you can prove sex discrimination. Let's say, for example, that Joan applies for a position as a resident apartment manager. She is told that the management wants a married couple. She returns with her friend Judy. She gets the job. Why? The EEOC says, "By limiting the two employees filling such positions to married couples . . . the employer . . . is discriminating against potential applicants of both sexes who may apply in pairs of persons of the same sex."[7] In other words, the policy discriminates on the basis of sex because it favors male-female pairs over male-male or female-female pairs. So the management may not reject same-sex couples. What would have happened if Joan had brought her friend Joe? She could not have demonstrated sex discrimination. She would have been in the same position as Kathleen Sullivan and

Neil Mindel and would have had to go to court on grounds of invasion of privacy—the right *not* to marry, if you will.

Can an Employer Inquire into Your Marital Status?

Generally, yes. The EEOC Sex Discrimination Guidelines, Section 3950.07, state: "A pre-employment inquiry may ask whether you are Mr., Mrs., or Miss provided the inquiry is made in good faith and for a non-discriminatory purpose." If you can demonstrate that because of your marital status you were not hired, then you can probably show that the inquiry was not made for a nondiscriminatory purpose.

The exception to the rule that an employer may ask your marital status is in the field of education. If the employer participates in an educational program that benefits from federal funds—and that is almost every institution—it may not inquire into your marital status under Section 86.60 of the EEOC Regulations promulgated June 4, 1975, effective July 21, 1975.

Can You Be Denied a Job or Fired Because You Are Married to a Co-Employee?

Yes, except, again, if the practice constitutes sex discrimination. Many employers prohibit the employment of relatives, especially husband and wife, at the same time. This is frequently true of school districts and universities. These rules are often called nepotism rules because they are designed to prevent an employee from being in a position to favor a spouse or a relative.

How do nepotism rules work? Ms. and Mr. Harper worked in the reservations department at TWA before they were married. When they married, she was dismissed under TWA's nepotism policy. The policy said that members of the same family were not permitted to work in the same department. The couple could elect who would resign, but if they did not decide, TWA would discharge the person with less seniority. Ms. Harper appealed her dismissal and tried to show that although the policy did not discriminate against women on its face, it did so in practice. But the court did not find her evidence convincing. The judge said that there were sound business reasons for the policy—such as the need to avoid double absences, conflicts of interest in promotional situations, and the possibility that their close proximity during working hours would be distracting.[8] Ms. Harper had a difficult argument to make. No doubt she tried to show that more women than men were dismissed as a result of this policy. One argument she could have raised is that the policy has a disparate impact on women because of their disadvantaged position in the labor market—they tend to earn less and have less seniority than men. So even though the couple has the choice of who leaves, they will tend to choose the one who makes less money—the woman. Similarly, when TWA has the choice, it dismisses the one with less seniority—more than likely, the woman. In this way, even a rule that is neutral on its face can be shown to result in sex discrimination.

The nepotism problem also arises where an employer prohibits the employment of a person whose spouse works for a competitive company. Mrs. Emory was dismissed from her job as a secretary with an insurance company when her husband got a job as a salesman with a competing health-insurance firm. Her company had a policy of not hiring or retaining a person whose spouse was employed by a competitor as protection against leakage of information that would be of benefit to the competitor. Ostensibly, the policy applied to both men and women. But Mrs. Emory discovered that a man whose wife worked with a competitor had not been made to leave. She appealed her dismissal based on sex discrimination. The company, however, then told the man he would have to go unless his wife gave up her job. So the court decided that the policy was applied equally to men and women and was not discriminatory. Ironically, the male employee had his wife quit her job, probably because he had a higher salary, and both women got the ax.[9]

Educational institutions are notorious for their nepotism policies. Until 1971, the State University of New York had a rule that prohibited the "parent, child, brother, sister, husband or wife of any member of the academic or nonacademic staff of any college" from appointment to any position at the same college. The policy came under attack in 1970 by Ms. Sanbonmatsu, a speech teacher at the State University of New York at Brockport. When she came to Brockport in 1964, she met Mr. Sanbonmatsu, also a member of the speech department. They married and she resigned pursuant to the rule. She was rehired as a temporary employee, which apparently didn't violate the rule, but which did not accord her fringe benefits and tenure rights. She requested full-time employment but was turned down because of the nepotism policy. In 1970, she applied for pregnancy leave. She was fired. Ms. Sanbonmatsu brough suit seeking reinstatement. She argued that the policy discriminated against her because of her sex. She demonstrated that out of twenty-seven husband/wife nepotism cases at Brockport, none of the men were required to accept temporary appointment. In some cases, wives were employed part-time and were truly temporary employees. In others, the wives worked full-time and the appointments were merely designated as temporary. The court decided that the rule had been applied unevenly and had resulted in discrimination against women. Ms. Sanbonmatsu was reinstated.

The most interesting thing about the case is that although it was decided on sex-discrimination grounds, the court also questioned the constitutionality of the nepotism policy. It said:

> it may be observed that freedom of personal choice in matters of marriage and family life is one of the rights protected by the Fourteenth Amendment to the U.S. Constitution. . . . Since classifications based upon marital status or familial relationships have little to do with teaching competency, one would expect that a nepotism rule which circumscribes employment practices on those grounds would require a powerful rationale to justify its existence.[10]

These constitutional arguments were raised unsuccessfully in another recent school case in which sex discrimination was not an issue. Edward Keckeisen had been the principal of Glenwood High School in Minnesota for three years. Lois Korbel had been the physical education teacher there for six years. In 1972, they were married. The school board had a policy prohibiting the employment of husband

and wife in an administrator-teacher relationship to avoid conflicts of interest. It was the school board's prerogative to decide who should go; it fired Mr. Keckeisen, presumably because he had less seniority. He appealed his dismissal on the grounds that it violated his right to marry as protected by the Ninth Amendment. The Court of Appeals said that the school board's policy did not violate his right to marry for two reasons: first, the right to marry is only indirectly affected—the main impact of the policy was to prohibit employment of married couples in administrator-teacher relationships; second, the policy, designed to prevent conflicts of interest and favoritism, is justified by the state's interest in providing good education for its children. The main problem the court saw was the deleterious effect on the morale of the faculty due to potential favoritism by an administrator to his teacher-spouse. In addition, it foresaw possible conflict of interest in mediation by an administrator between his wife and a student and possible favoritism in obtaining school supplies. The court said that such conflicts are subversive of the state's interest in good education.[11]

The court itself gave some inkling of what would have made it reach a different decision. It said, "Were the right to marriage claim not so attenuated by the fact that marriage itself is not the subject of the Board's policy, i.e. were the right more directly involved—then we should perhaps reach a different result."[12] Yet the policy singles out the married couple in its presumption of potential favoritism. For all other relationships, the Board may take action only where a conflict of interest actually occurs. Is it not reasonable to think that a parent-child or sibling-sibling relationship would engender equal opportunity for favoritism? By singling out the married couple when in fact all close relationships place the participants equally in a possible conflict-of-interest situation, the policy reveals that its subject *is* marriage, contrary to what the court concluded.

In addition, the court said:

> It must be noted that appellant [Keckeisen] did not offer any evidence at the hearing and he has failed to inform the court of any possible alternatives by which appellees might have served the state's interests in eliminating conflicts of interest. . . . Had appellant showed some reasonable alternatives of accomplishing the same result, this court might have found the incidental burden on the right to marriage to be, in balance, greater than the burden on the state.[13]

It would have been wise litigation strategy for Keckeisen to have shown that the conflicts of interest and favoritism can be avoided by less broad measures than the blanket prohibition on marriage. For instance, why couldn't the same standards applied to other relatives be applied to a married couple—when a problem arises, the individuals disqualify themselves or are disqualified from taking action by the Board. The problem here is that the Board's means of avoiding conflicts of interest and favoritism could be achieved by less broad measures that would not infringe on the right to marry. For instance, the school district could adopt a policy of hiring married couples but prohibiting them from participating in a decision concerning promotion, salary, or termination of a close relative or spouse.

Can You Be Excluded from a Professional Association Because You Are Living with Someone?

Membership in professional associations or a license to practice certain professions is conditional on the applicant's demonstration of his/her moral fitness. Moral fitness must be demonstrated to obtain law, medical, teaching, and liquor licenses and security clearances. Where "morality" is in question, the licensing body may deny your application because of your cohabitation out of wedlock. However, homosexual behavior has more often been the basis for denial of these licenses than cohabitation or fornication. The only cases in which one is likely to be denied admission to the bar or disbarred for private heterosexual activity involve some flagrance—such as an attorney who impregnates his young stepdaughter —or have some connection with the practice of law —such as an attorney who has an affair with his client's wife.[14]

Where "morality" is an issue, you may be asked some personal questions. The application for the bar for the Second Department in New York State has asked the names of the people with whom you are living and their relationship to you. Not only does this information have a questionable relationship to your ability to practice a profession, but it may also be an invasion of your rights to privacy and freedom of association. The organizations would argue that membership is a privilege, not a right, and therefore they may screen applicants as they wish. In response, we may argue that no licensing group that, in effect, acts for the state may condition receipt of its benefits upon the sacrifice of a constitutional right. One caveat: If you make false statements on your application, you can lose your license on grounds of perjury.

The chance that you will be excluded from a profession because you are living with someone is slim. It is greater if you live in a state where cohabitation or fornication is a crime. Generally, conviction of a crime renders one ineligible for membership in certain professions. In states where cohabitation or fornication is a crime, even though you may not have been convicted, an association or licensing body may consider your behavior criminal and, therefore, immoral. In other words, living together would be prima facie evidence of immorality. This is not likely to occur if you are fairly discreet and don't mix business with pleasure.

If you are about to be expelled from an association for living with someone and can demonstrate that your living arrangement did not adversely affect your professional performance, you have a better case than if you were never a member in the first place, because you have a vested property right in your membership.

Can You Be Denied a Job or Fired Because You Are an Unwed Mother?

The best reading of the law is no. In 1970, the EEOC decided that a company's policy of refusing to hire unwed mothers discriminates against women and is therefore unlawful under Title VII of the 1964 Civil Rights Act. Let's say Paula, who is pregnant and unmarried, and Paul, whose girlfriend is pregnant by him, are seeking the same job. She is a potential unwed mother; he is a potential unwed father. Who gets the job, assuming all else is equal? The EEOC said that even if the employer refused to hire unwed mothers *and* unwed fathers, the policy would still tend to deprive women of jobs more often than men because: "Bearing a child out of wedlock is a fact not easily hidden from an employer's discovery procedures, whereas it's a wise employer indeed that knows which of its male applicants truthfully answered its illegitimacy inquiry."[15]

A Mississippi school district had a policy of treating unwed parenthood as prima facie proof of immorality and summarily dismissed a teacher because she had illegitimate children. The policy was based on the notion that unwed parents are improper role models for students and that their presence in a school contributed to pregnancy among schoolgirls. The Fifth Circuit Court of Appeals said that there was no evidence that this was true. It said that before a woman could be dismissed, she had to be given a public hearing regarding her "immorality" and the right to appeal or her Fourteenth Amendment right to due process would be violated.[16] At the hearing, the board would have to demonstrate that her unwed motherhood had an adverse effect on the students, which would be difficult to do. The case was appealed to the Supreme Court, but after hearing arguments, the Court decided to withdraw certiorari as "improvidently granted." (See page 21, note 4.) Therefore, the circuit court opinion remains in effect.

Can You Be Dismissed from the Military for Living Together?

Yes. The Uniform Code of Military Justice, which governs all the armed services, has two applicable sections—Articles 133 and 134. Article 133 says that anyone who is convicted of conduct unbecoming an officer and a gentleman shall be punished as a court-martial may direct. Article 134 says that all conduct of a nature to bring discredit upon the armed forces or to the prejudice of good order and discipline in the armed forces shall be punished at the discretion of a court-martial. These nonspecific provisions open the door for dismissal or punishment for living together. To my knowledge, there have been no dismissals for this reason. However, other rules have been used to deny promotions because a man and a woman were living together. A female second lieutenant and a male private first class met while the former was a nurse and the latter a medical technician in an army hospital in Germany. They began living together. They were both denied promotions apparently on the basis of rules prohibiting fraternization between officers and enlisted personnel.[17] They left the military of their own accord, but if they hadn't, they might well have been dismissed.

NOTES

1. *Sullivan* v. *Meade County Independent School District*, 387 F. Supp. 1237 (D.C. S. Dak. 1975).
2. *Mindel* v. *U.S. Civil Service Commission*, 312 F. Supp. 485 (N.D. Cal. 1970).

3. EEOC Decision No. 71–2678, June 28, 1971.

4. *Williams* v. *United States,* 434 F.2d 1346 (1970).

5. *Sprogis* v. *United Air Lines,* 444 F.2d 1194 (7th Cir. 1971); *Lansdale* v. *United Air Lines,* 437 F.2d 454 (5th Cir. 1971).

6. EEOC Decision No. 71–2613, 4 Fair Employment Practices (F.E.P.) Cases 22, June 22, 1971.

7. 4 F.E.P. Cases 253, July 7, 1971.

8. *Harper* v. *Trans World Airlines, Inc.,* 385 F. Supp. 1001 (E.D. Mo. 1974), affirmed on appeal, 525 F.2d 409 (8th Cir. 1975).

9. *Judith B. Emory* v. *Georgia Hospital Services Administration,* 4 F.E.P. Cases 891, April 31, 1971.

10. *Sanbonmatsu* v. *Boyer,* 45 A.D.2d 249, 251, 252; 357 N.Y.S.2d 245 (1974).

11. *Keckeisen* v. *Independent School District 612,* 509 F.2d 1062 (8th Cir. 1975); cert. denied October 7, 1975, 44 United States Law Week 3202.

12. *Keckeisen* v. *Independent School District 612,* p. 1065.

13. *Ibid.,* p. 1066.

14. See 36 American Law Reports 3d 735.

15. 2 F.E.P. Cases 1016, September 28, 1970.

16. *Andrews* v. *Drew Municipal School District,* 507 F.2d 611 (5th Cir. 1975). The U.S. Supreme Court granted certiorari April 21, 1975, Docket No. 74–1318, but on May 3, 1976, dismissed the case.

17. *New York Times,* August 31, 1974.

9 / Taxation

In April 1974, a very unusual demonstration occurred on the steps of St. Patrick's Cathedral in New York. Anita and Christopher Murray, married to each other for six years, were "remarried" in a mock ceremony replete with priest and Mendelssohn. This time, however, they carried a placard that read, in large letters, "This wedding cost $3,000," and in smaller letters, "in taxes." The Murrays were protesting what has come to be known as the TCM—the tax cost of marriage. A husband and wife who both generate income pay more federal income tax than two single people with the same combined income. The Murrays computed that since the present tax rates became effective, they paid $1,000 more per year in income tax than they would have if they had been single. At that rate, they could live together unwed not only for fun, but also for profit.

In 1971, Vivien Kellems, an unmarried taxpayer, sent a letter to the secretary of the treasury billing the government for about $76,000. This amount, she said, represented the taxes the IRS had exacted from her over a twenty-year period, plus interest, just because she couldn't find a husband. Until 1969, when the tax laws were amended, a single person could pay up to 40 percent higher taxes than a one-income married couple filing jointly that had the same income. Since then, a single person may still pay up to 20 percent higher taxes than his/her married counterpart.

So you see that the present tax system is a paradox. Single people pay a higher tax than one-income married people filing jointly. But two-incomed married people filing jointly (or separately) pay a higher tax than an unmarried couple with the same income. The tax system favors married people when one of the spouses does not work outside the home. It likes unmarried people less. It likes married people when both spouses work outside the home least of all. Nowhere will you find a more clear, or more subtle, expression of the value our society places on marriage and on the stay-at-home wife. Yet during 1974, an average of 53 percent of all women between the ages of eighteen and sixty-four were in the labor force and some 58 percent of those women who work are married with husbands present.[1]

What Is the TCM?

The TCM is the difference between the tax paid by a married couple when both husband and wife work outside the home (i.e., have income) and the tax paid by an unmarried couple with the same income. The easiest way to understand TCM is by example. Let's examine the tax liability of an unmarried and a married couple each with two incomes for 1974. Angela and Michael are unmarried and living together. Angela earns $15,000 a year as a legal services lawyer; Michael earns $25,000 a year as a lawyer in private practice. Maria and Joseph are married. Maria earns $15,000 a year as a teacher;

Joseph earns $25,000 a year as a real estate broker.
Let's assume, for the sake of simplicity, that each
couple takes the standard deduction (15 percent of
gross income or $2,000, whichever is less). Angela
and Michael pay a federal income tax of $9,310.
Maria and Joseph, who have the same combined
income but who are married, pay $11,240 if they
file jointly or $11,680 if they file separately. Maria
and Joseph pay $1,930 to $2,370 more. What
accounts for the disparity?

There are two reasons. First, Angela and Michael
may take a standard deduction—$2,000 plus $2,000
is subtracted from their gross income; but Maria and
Joseph may take only one standard deduction between the two of them—if they file jointly, $2,000
is subtracted from their combined gross income; if
they file separately, $1,000 (half the maximum
standard deduction) is subtracted from each of their
incomes—so their *taxable* income is greater.

Second, the marginal rates applied to married–
filing-jointly and married–filing-separately are higher
than those for single people.[2] You will see why by
following how their taxes are computed. Angela's tax
is computed as follows: Her gross income is $15,000.
She deducts the maximum allowable standard deduction ($2,000) and gets a taxable income of $13,000.
Under the proper Internal Revenue Code table, she
must pay $2,630 plus 29 percent of $1,000, which
comes to $2,920 in tax. Her marginal rate is 29
percent. Michael's tax is computed using the same
table. His gross income is $25,000. He subtracts his
standard deduction ($2,000) and gets a taxable
income of $23,000. His tax is $5,990 plus 40 percent
of $1,000, which comes to $6,390. His marginal rate

is 40 percent. Angela and Michael's combined tax bill is $9,310.

Maria and Joseph's tax is computed using a different table. When people are married and file a joint return, their income is combined. Maria's income ($15,000) plus Joseph's income ($25,000) comes to $40,000. Then the single standard deduction ($2,000) allowed them is subtracted to get their taxable income, $38,000. Their tax is $10,340 plus 45 percent of $2,000, which comes to $11,240. Their marginal rate is 45 percent, higher than either Angela's or Michael's. The TCM to Maria and Joseph is $11,240 minus $9,310, which comes to $1,930.

If Maria and Joseph filed separately, their taxes would be computed as follows. Maria's taxable income is $15,000 minus $1,000 (one half the standard deduction), or $14,000. Using the proper table, her tax is $2,830 plus 36 percent of $2,000, or $3,650. Joseph's taxable income is $25,000 minus $1,000, or $24,000. His tax is $7,030 plus 50 percent of $2,000, or $8,030. Their combined tax bill is $11,680. The tax cost to them of filing separately is $440; the tax cost of marriage is $2,370.

The tax cost of marriage roughly increases as income increases, because we have a progressive tax structure in which higher incomes are taxed at higher rates.[3]

The 1975 Tax Reduction Act will have a slight remedial effect on the TCM. The act establishes different standard deductions for married and single people. A married couple filing jointly will be entitled to take one deduction of $2,300. Until the act, the standard deduction was the same for both married and single people. In theory, the standard deduction represents what it costs to live for a year. (Of course, this is a fiction, since it obviously costs much more to live than $2,300 per year.) The new law reflects the attitude that although two cannot live *as* cheaply as one, it costs only about 15 percent more per year for two. At least it is a step in the direction of realizing that a married couple should not have to share one meager standard deduction between them. Ideally, each spouse should be able to take his/her own. Beyond the fact that the Tax Reduction Act does not go far enough to remedy the TCM, keep in mind that it has been enacted for 1975 only. Unless it is extended sometime in 1976, we will be back to the same deduction for a married couple and a single individual.

Can You Avoid the TCM by Divorcing and Remarrying Every Year?

Technically, yes, but it is not a good idea. One Chicago couple, both CPA's each earning $22,500 per year, is reported to have done this.[4] To determine whether you may file as married or single for a given tax year, the IRS looks at your marital status as of December 31. This couple obtained a divorce in late December so that they could file as single in that tax year. They remarried in early January and plan to divorce again in December. Their tax savings exceeded the costs of their divorce and remarriage. This procedure is highly impractical and is not recommended for several reasons. First, this kind of divorce is collusive. If a court saw through your plan, it would probably deny the divorce and suggest you remedy the tax inequity through the legislature. Second, what if you agreed to divorce and remarry for tax reasons but one of you reneged? A court would probably not enforce your agreement because it is designed to induce divorce, which courts don't like. Third, what if one of you dies between the divorce and remarriage? You would lose your right as spouse to claim a portion of the estate (the spousal election) and in many states any provision for a spouse in a will is rendered null and void by a divorce. You can provide for each other by stating in a will, "I give Veronica Hart my entire estate whether or not she is my wife when I die," but few people have the foresight or energy to do this. Fourth, if you have children, all these problems are compounded. Finally, sidestepping the tax does not eliminate the inequity.

When Is It Cheaper, in Terms of Taxes, to Be Married? What Is the Tax Cost of Being Single?

In terms of taxes, it is cheaper to be married if only one spouse has income and you file jointly. In other words, a married couple in which only one spouse generates income pays a lower tax on the same income than a single person. To use our sample couples again, if Maria had no income and Joseph earned $25,000 a year, his tax would be $4,380 plus 32 percent of $3,000, $5,340. Michael, who also earns $25,000 a year but who is unmarried, would face a higher tax. His tax would be $5,990 plus 40 percent of $1,000, or $6,390. So the tax cost of being single is $1,050. Single people pay up to 20 percent more than a one-income married couple with the same income.

The difference occurs because the rate table used for married–filing-jointly has a built-in "income-splitting" factor. That means that Joseph's income is treated as if one half had been earned by Joseph and the other half by Maria. Let's say Joseph earns $25,000 and Maria earns nothing. We subtract the standard deduction ($2,000) and get $23,000 in taxable income. In effect, the rate table says each spouse must pay tax on one half the income, so their total tax is two times the tax on $11,500. Because we have a progressive tax structure—meaning the higher the income, the higher the rate at which it is taxed—the tax rate on $11,500 is lower than the one on $23,000. Therefore, when you multiply the tax on $11,500 by two it remains lower than the tax on $23,000. Thus Joseph and Maria pay a lower tax than Michael.

The income-splitting factor is not available to one-income married couples filing separately. If Maria (no income) and Joseph ($25,000 income) filed separately, their tax would be $8,030, higher that it would be if they filed jointly and higher than Michael's tax.

What Is the Origin of the Present Inequities?

Traditionally, in community property states each spouse had an equal share in all income that came into the marriage. Husbands and wives in those states were therefore allowed to split the total income in half, so that each paid tax on one half the income. That gave citizens in community property states a tax advantage over citizens in separate property states, because the tax rate on one half an amount is lower than the rate on the total amount. Married citizens in separate property states protested their disadvantage. In 1948, Congress enacted a rate table to correct the disparity. The new table, applicable to married citizens filing jointly, had a built-in income-splitting factor. But it created a new inequity—single persons paid up to 40 percent higher taxes than married persons filing jointly who had the same total income. As a result, in 1969, Congress again enacted a new rate table. This time it reduced the possible disparity between singles and married–filing-jointly to a maximum of 20 percent. The new rates made single people less angry, although not happy. But the new table created another inequity—between married people with two incomes and unmarried couples with the same combined income. It also left married people filing separately with the pre-1948 rate. Even when the rates were lowered for single people, those for married–filing-separately remained the same. Legislators feared that if married people were permitted to use the new single rates, they could divide their income so that they paid less than if they filed jointly. That could occur when both spouses had income. Although such a practice would reduce tax revenue, it would eliminate the TCM for two-income married couples.

*How Could the Inequity between the Two-Income
Married Couple and the Unmarried Couple
with the Same Combined Income Be Remedied?*

The establishment of a per capita standard deduction would partially remedy the problem. A married couple should be able to take two standard deductions instead of one between them.

In addition, married people could be given the option of using the singles rates. That would put the two-income married couple on a par with their unmarried counterparts.

However, the two-income married couple would still be deprived of the benefit the one-income married couple receives. Why? Because the one-income couple, in effect, "underreports" income. How? When a wife works in the home, she provides services that are of economic benefit to the family. She cares for children, cooks, cleans, sews, decorates, entertains, and more. But these benefits to the family are not included in its tax base. On the other hand, if a wife works outside the home, the economic benefit of her services—her income—is included in the tax base. Not only must she pay taxes, but she may also have to pay someone to perform the services she would have performed had she remained in the home. It is impractical to tax the value of the services performed by the wife who works in the home, because her efforts do not generate money. However, it is feasible to equalize the treatment of wives who work outside the home with that of wives who work in the home. How? By providing a tax benefit to the wife who works outside the home in the form of a deduction from earned income for expenses incurred in order to permit her to be gainfully employed. The child-care deduction is a first, although imperfect, step in this direction.

How Could the Inequity between Single People and One-Income Married People Be Remedied?

By abandoning income splitting and by going to a system of individual taxation regardless of marital status. But this remedy is nowhere in sight. The courts are not yet even at the point where they question whether marriage should be a favored status or not.

The tax penalty on being single has been challenged in the courts by Vivien Kellems as a violation of the Fourteenth Amendment, among others. She argued that there was no rational basis for treating single and married people differently. But the U.S. Tax Court decided that there was a rational basis for treating single and married people differently.[5] Why? First, the need to equalize tax treatment of married people in community and separate property states; second, the recognition of the greater financial burdens of married people. The judge did not define what these greater burdens on the married taxpayer are.

Do married people bear greater financial burdens than single people? Not necessarily. In fact, there are certain economies of scale: to the extent that married people share goods and services, they can live, per capita, more cheaply than single people. For example, they may share rent, furnishings, and perhaps food. Aside from these costs, most costs are a function of the individual and not the marital unit —e.g., medical care, clothing, transportation. So married people would tend to have expenses equal to or less than similarly situated single people. What the judge may be envisioning when he speaks of the higher costs of marriage is the marriage in which the husband is the sole breadwinner. And when there are children, he may reason that a wife (and children) is an expensive proposition. It is not marriage, however, that makes her expensive, but the fact that she is dependent.

We may even question whether the dependent wife is expensive at all. In fact she is a rather good deal. It is estimated that the value of her work may be as high as $13,400 per year if there are children and around $8,800 per year if there are none.[6]

There may be some rational bases for treating married and single people differently, but a greater financial burden does not appear to be one of them. Any greater financial burden experienced by an individual is a function of the number of dependents and the costs each incurs, not the fact of marriage. That burden should be adjusted by deductions, not income splitting.

Can You Claim the Person You Live with as a Dependent on Your Income Tax Return?

No. The IRS already thought of that one. The statute says you may take a deduction for certain members of your household. But it then says: "An individual is not a member of the taxpayer's household if at any time during the taxable year . . . the relationship between such individual and the taxpayer is in violation of local law."[7] Cohabitation is not in violation of local law in every state, you say, so why can't I claim him/her where it isn't illegal? Unfortunately, although it seems unreasonable, the IRS has decided that the statute doesn't mean what it says; rather, it means that people who are living together cannot claim each other as dependents. Period. The issue seems ripe for challenge.

What Is the Household Expenses and Child-Care Deduction? Is It Available to Single People?

The Internal Revenue Code permits a person who maintains a household for a "qualifying individual" to deduct expenses he/she incurs in order to be gainfully employed. The deduction is available to married and single people. But it has many restrictive qualifications.

First, maintaining a household means you must furnish over half the cost of maintaining it for that year. Second, a "qualifying individual" is (1) a child under fifteen for whom the taxpayer can take a dependency exemption, or (2) a spouse or other dependent of the taxpayer who is physically or mentally incapable of caring for him/herself. In effect, the provision requiring the child under fifteen to be the taxpayer's legal dependent precludes many divorced women from taking the deduction. Why? Because the former husband usually claims the child as a dependent even though the former wife has custody and must cope with child care. Also, a person who hires a housecleaner or a cook in order to be gainfully employed but who does not have a "qualifying individual" cannot take the deduction.

Third, to take advantage of the deduction a married couple must file jointly (except if the taxpayer's spouse was absent for the entire tax year). We have already seen how the joint-return rate structure hurts married people with two incomes; in addition, the joint-return requirement can prove difficult for a person who becomes divorced, separated, or married during the year.

Fourth, the taxpayer must itemize his/her deductions. Most taxpayers, especially those in the lower-income brackets, use the standard deduction. Therefore it is generally only mid- to upper-bracket taxpayers who benefit from the deduction.

Fifth, the expenses must be incurred so as to enable the taxpayer to be *gainfully* employed. No deduction is allowed if you are doing volunteer work.

Sixth, no deduction is available for payments made to relatives.

Seventh, there is a limit on how much you can deduct. You can deduct a maximum of $400 a month ($4,800 a year) for expenses incurred in the home, e.g., housecleaning and dependent care. But you may deduct a different amount if the care of the "qualifying individual" is provided outside the home: up to $200 a month for one child, up to $300 a month for two, up to $400 a month for three or more.

Finally, there is a limit on how much you can earn in order to take the deduction. As of March 1975, the income limit was raised from $18,000 to $35,000 per year. Now, if your income is $35,000 or less you may deduct the maximum $400 a month. If your income exceeds $35,000 per year, the amount of expenses you may deduct must be reduced by 50¢ for every dollar over $35,000 allocable to the month in which the expenses were incurred. For example, if you earned $36,200, there would be $1,200 in excess of $35,000, or $100 per month; so you must reduce your deduction for any given month by $50. If a taxpayer has an income of over $44,600, no deduction is allowed.

How Is the Household Expenses and Child-Care Deduction Relevant to Single People Who Live Together?

It is relevant in that it makes some distinctions based on marital status that make it to your advantage to be single, assuming you have a "qualifying individual" (in most cases, a child). (Note that you cannot take a deduction based on each other.)

First, if you are married, both spouses' incomes are tabulated in determing whether you fall under the income limit. If you are merely living together, only the income of the person who is seeking the deduction is counted. Thus a married couple earning a combined income of $44,600 would be completely ineligible, while an unmarried couple each of whom earned almost that much would be eligible.

Second, if you are married, both husband and wife must be employed on a substantially full-time basis (at least thirty hours). Yet if you are unmarried, the taxpayer seeking the deduction need be employed only part-time.

Can You Be Held Liable for the Taxes of the Person with Whom You Are Living? Can You Be if You Are Married?

Unmarried taxpayers who live together cannot file jointly and cannot be held liable for each other's taxes. People who live in a common-law marriage state and who fulfill its requirements for common-law marriage are legally married and may file a joint return.

A husband and wife are jointly and severally liable if they file a joint return. That means that either or both of them can be held responsible for the entire tax, regardless of who earned the money. But the Internal Revenue Code offers some relief to an "innocent spouse." A spouse is relieved of liability if (1) the omission is attributable to the other spouse and exceeds 25 percent of the gross income shown on the return, (2) the spouse shows that he/she did not know and had no reason to know of the omission, and (3) under all the facts, including whether or not he/she had received significant benefit from the omitted item(s), his/her liability would be inequitable.[8] This provision benefits women because, more often than not, their husbands prepare the joint tax return.

A husband and wife who file separate returns cannot be held liable for each other's taxes.

NOTES

1. U.S. Department of Labor, Employment Standards Administration, Women's Bureau, *1975 Handbook on Women Workers*, Bulletin No. 297 (Washington, D.C., 1974), p. 3.
2. The marginal rate is the rate at which income above the "base income" is taxed. It varies from 15 to 70 percent and is often referred to as your tax "bracket."

The base income is the amount determined by the code that receives a lower tax rate. It varies with income level and filing table.

3. According to Joyce M. Nussbaum, there is a tendency for the TCM to increase as the wife's share of family income increases, although it declines somewhat after reaching a peak in the vicinity of 40 percent of family income. See Joyce M. Nussbaum, "The Tax Structure and Discrimination vs. Working Wives," *National Tax Journal* 25 (1972), pp. 183, 191, for a detailed discussion.

4. *New York Times,* March 27, 1975.

5. *Kellems* v. *Commissioner,* 58 U.S.T.C. 556 (1972). The decision was upheld by the Circuit Court of Appeals (474 F.2d 1399 [2nd Cir. 1973]) and was denied certiorari (414 U.S. 831 [1973]). The case was reappealed, but Ms. Kellems died before it could be completed.

6. Estimated by the Chase Manhattan Bank. Cited in Ann Crittenden Scott, "The Value of Housework: For Love or Money?" *Ms.,* July 1972, p. 59.

7. Internal Revenue Code of 1954, § 152(b) (5).

8. *Ibid.,* § 6013(e).

10 / Your Legal Name

Catherine and Anthony enclosed a card in the invitation to their wedding reception that said, "After marriage, Catherine will retain the surname McNulty." Nevertheless, they received gifts addressed to "Mr. and Mrs. Anthony Golden." Although Catherine had expressly communicated her intent to retain her name, many people refused to accept her decision. The tradition that a woman adopts the surname of her husband upon marriage is *that* strong. But is it law?

Must a Woman Take Her Husband's Surname upon Marriage?

At common law, a person acquires a name by repute. You may adopt any name you wish as long as it's not for a fraudulent purpose, e.g., to deceive your creditors or escape prosecution. But many state courts have assumed that the tradition that a wife adopt her husband's surname was law. Now, like other areas of the law, this one is in flux and difficult to assess. No state requires the name change by statute.[1] Only one state, Alabama, definitely requires the name change by case law.[2]

In the fifteen states that have enacted equal rights

amendments, the answer is clearly no, the name change is *not* required by law.[3] A recent Hawaii case bears out this interpretation: Hawaii had a statute that required that a woman take her husband's surname upon marriage. Leanne Cragun and Penelope Spiller sought to vote in their birth-given names and asserted that the statute denied them equal protection. The judge invalidated the statute. He reasoned that a statute that differentiates between the relative rights of men and women on as broad a scale as this for no reason except custom and usage denies equal protection.[4] Opinions of the attorneys general of various other states that have enacted equal rights amendments bear this out.[5]

The law in the remaining thirty-four states is difficult to determine. The basic issue is whether a woman's adopting her husband's surname is just a tradition or whether it is required by law. Since there are no statutes expressly requiring the name change, the answer to the question is based on how a court interprets prior judicial decisions. The courts of several states have spoken on the issue.[6] If you live in a state that regards the name change as a mere tradition, then you may legally retain your name after marriage. The major problem you will have is convincing other people that this is so. If you live in a state that regards the name change as legally required, you will have to petition the court to change your name back to your birth-given name. You will have to do this even if you have never used your husband's surname. Although it seems unfair, the U.S. Supreme Court has decided that requiring women to go through this procedure is not unduly burdensome.[7]

Only two states have enacted statutes expressly

permitting women to retain their birth-given surnames after marriage.[8]

If you live in a state where neither the legislature, nor the attorney general, nor the courts have spoken, you are in an uncertain position. Should you petition the court for a name change (back to your birth-given name even though you may never have used your husband's surname) or should you just continue to use your birth-given name as if you were single? The latter seems to make the most sense. The best view of English and American common law seems to be that the name change on marriage is a mere tradition and not legally required.[9] Going to court is costly no matter what people say. However, if you run into difficulty, yours may be the definitive test case for your state.

Why Would a Woman Wish Not to Change Her Name on Marriage?

In another culture, we would ask why a woman would wish to change her name. In fact, even in Western culture, the woman was not always the one to change her name. English husbands were known to take the wife's surname if her name was more eminent or in danger of extinction.

The name change has its origin in the supposed unity of husband and wife that resulted from marriage. With the enactment of the Married Women's Property Acts in the late nineteenth century, which made a wife a separate legal person from her husband, the concept of this unity was rendered obsolete. But the symbol of the supposed unity persists. A woman today may not wish to take her husband's surname for several reasons, both practical and psychological. She may already be known in her profession by a certain name and may damage her career by a name change. She may not wish to be identified in terms of her husband. She may also reject the gender-based distinction that it is women, not men, who customarily change their names. If the two people feel they want to share the same name, it would be less discriminatory for each to add on the other's name or to adopt a name new to both of them.

If You Wish to Retain Your Name after Marriage, What Should You Do?

Use it exclusively. Build a record showing your intent to retain your name. Include a statement to that effect in your wedding announcement, obtain identification after your marriage in your birth name, or execute a written antenuptial agreement signed by you and your husband that says, for example, "In consideration of marriage, Catherine McNulty and Anthony Golden agree that Catherine McNulty will not adopt the name Golden and will retain her birth-given surname for all purposes after their marriage." Try to stop people from addressing you by your husband's surname. Indeed, there are limits—you're great uncle or aunt may never understand—but remind the people with whom you have daily dealings that your name is Catherine McNulty, not Mrs. Golden. You will meet resistance, but you do have legal support for your position. If your state has a statute that permits you to petition the court to *establish* your name (e.g., Wisconsin), you may do so if you wish judicial confirmation of your practice.

If you retain your birth name for professional purposes only, you create the problem for others of defining what is professional and what is personal. As a practical matter, you must be prepared to have a court tell you at some point what your legal name is in the context in which the issue is raised.

If You Have Used Your Husband's Surname but Wish to Change Back to Your Birth-Given Name, What Do You Do?

If you are still married, then you can either just resume using your birth name or, if you wish, petition the court for a name change. Resume using your birth name by changing all your identification— credit cards, voter registration, insurance policies, employer identification number records, school registration, passport, and professional licenses. You may wish to send an announcement to all the people with whom you have contact in your professional and personal life—for example, "Mary Smith Jones announces that she will be known as Mary Smith as of July 1, 1975." But you *must* inform your creditors of the change.

If you wish greater certainty, you may petition the court for a name change.

If you are divorced, the divorce decree may indicate, as it must in New York, that you are authorized to resume the use of your maiden name.[10] If it does not, you may either just resume using your maiden name or petition the court to modify the decree. A California court has recently held that the mere presence of minor children is not a substantial enough reason to deny the divorced woman's request to resume her maiden name.[11]

In What Situations May Problems Using Your Birth-Given Name Arise if You Are Married?

Problems may arise when you run for office, register to vote, apply for a driver's license, are sued, seek to be naturalized, apply for credit or to renew your passport. Generally, you will be on strongest ground if you have written evidence that you have kept your name for all purposes—e.g., your contract, marriage announcement, or postmarriage identification.

In What Situations May Problems with Your Name Arise if You Are Unmarried and Living Together?

An unmarried woman has the right to use the name of the man she is living with, or any other name for that matter. (See page 160.) But if she does, she may run into two types of problems. First, if you live in a state that recognizes common-law marriage, you run the risk of having a marriage and all its obligations imposed upon you by the state. (See Chapter 2, page 24.) While use of the man's surname is not conclusive proof of common-law marriage, it is one persuasive indication. Second, you may be found to use the man's surname for a fraudulent purpose—for example, if someone has extended credit to you because of your representation that you are married and he/she suffers some financial loss, you will be held liable. So be careful.

If the landlord wants you to sign as Mrs. Jones, don't. Tell the landlord that even if you were married you wouldn't have to use the same name. If his/her problem is that he/she does not want to rent to single people, then the matter should be taken up under local housing-discrimination statutes. (See pages 85–86.)

Do You Have to Use Miss, Mr., Mrs., or Ms.?

No. These prefixes are mere titles. They describe an individual by sex and, for Miss/Mrs., marital status. But they are not part of a name. If an application form asks for such a title, you are not obligated to supply it. The Arkansas federal court has held that it is unconstitutional to require women registering to vote to use "Miss" or "Mrs."[12]

What Is the Status of the Title "Ms."?

According to *Ms.* magazine, the title "Ms." appeared in secretarial handbooks as early as the 1940's as a way to address a woman whose marital status was unknown. Like the other prefixes, "Ms." has no particular legal import.

NOTES

1. Puerto Rico has such a statute (Title 31, § 287).

2. *Forbush* v. *Wallace,* 341 F. Supp. 217 (M.D. Ala. 1971), affirmed per curiam, 415 U.S. 970 (1972).

3. Alaska, Colorado, Connecticut, Hawaii, Illinois, Maryland, Massachusetts, Montana, New Mexico, Pennsylvania, Texas, Utah, Virginia, Washington, Wyoming.

4. *Cragun* v. *Hawaii & Kashimoto,* Civ. No. 43175 1st Cir. Ct., Hawaii, January 27, 1975, Women Law Reporter, March 1, 1975.

5. Texas (Opinion No. 432, October 25, 1974), Illinois (Opinion No. S-711, February 25, 1974), Pennsylvania (Opinions No. 62, October 25, 1973, and No. 8, January 31, 1974), Women Law Reporter, November 15, 1974.

6. Wisconsin, New York, Tennessee, and Arkansas are among those that do not require the name change upon marriage. See Priscilla R. MacDougall, "Kruzel: A Landmark Names Case," Women Law Reporter, May 1, 1975.

7. *Forbush* v. *Wallace,* n. 2.

8. Massachusetts (which has an ERA) and Minnesota.

9. Priscilla R. MacDougall, "Married Women's Common Law Right to Their Own Surname," *Women's Rights Law Reporter* 1, no. 3 (Fall–Winter 1972–1973), p. 2.

10. N.Y.S. Domestic Relations Law § 240–a (McKinney's 1964).

11. *In re Marriage of Banks,* 42 C.A.3d 631, 117 Cal. Rptr. 37 (1974).

12. *Walker et al.* v. *Jackson,* 391 F. Supp. 1395 (D.C. Ark. 1975).

11 / Domicile

Linda and Chris have been living together in New York for three years. They are thinking of getting married this spring. Linda applied to medical school for admission in the fall. Because the competition is great, she applied to schools all over the country, as well as New York. She would prefer to stay in New York, but the only school to which she has been accepted is in Kansas. She has decided to go there and would like to establish a domicile in Kansas because she would then be eligible for the low tuition rates for people domiciled in Kansas. ("Domicile" is explained in the next section, below.) Furthermore, she expects that she will be there for at least six years and would like to become a part of the community for other purposes as well. Chris has a one-year contract to teach sculpture at a New York school. Such a position is hard to come by and he does not wish to abandon it, nor is it to his advantage to breach his contract. Linda and Chris view their anticipated separation as temporary. As soon as Chris's contract is fulfilled, he will join Linda in Kansas. Should they get married this spring or wait another year?

If the law of domicile were the only consideration, they would be better off waiting a year until Chris could join Linda in Kansas. Why? Because, in

Kansas, as in many other states, a wife's domicile is that of her husband. If they were married, Linda would be considered to be domiciled in New York even though she would be living in Kansas; therefore she would be unable to establish a domicile in Kansas and would be ineligible for the lower tuition rates. If Chris were going to medical school in Kansas, he could become domiciled in Kansas and avail himself of the lower tuition rates, even if his wife remained in New York. If Linda remains unmarried, she can establish a domicile in Kansas.

This is but one example of the way in which the law of domicile discriminates against married women and, indirectly, their husbands as well, since presumably both will bear the burden of the greater tuition fee. It demonstrates, also, one way in which the law of domicile may enter into the decision to marry.

What Is Meant by the Term "Domicile"? Is It the Same as "Residence"?

"Domicile" is a legal term that denotes the one place in which a person intends to remain or to return to. The determination of domicile is made on analyzing factors that manifest that intent. Among the factors a court will consider are where you vote, where you pay your taxes, where you maintain your primary residence (as opposed to a vacation home), and where you work. No one factor is definitive.[1] "Domicile" is not synonymous with "residence." For example, a student may reside in California while attending school, yet be domiciled in New York. A businessperson may maintain an apartment in

Chicago, where he or she resides for long periods of time, yet his/her domicile may be elsewhere.

Why Is Your Domicile Important?

It is important because it determines where you can vote and hold office; where you are eligible for state scholarships or lower tuition fees, welfare benefits, and jury service; where your estate will be probated. It is also important because it affects whether you can sue or be sued in a specific federal court and which state court may adjudicate your case in a divorce or child-custody matter.

What Does Domicile Have to Do with Living Together?

The mere fact that you are living with another person outside of marriage has no effect on your domicile. But for married couples, in most states and for most purposes the wife's domicile would be that of her husband. Therefore a married woman may find herself deprived of certain rights and privileges if she moves out of the state of her husband's domicile. Knowing that, two people who are living together may decide not to marry.

What Is the Origin of the General Rule that a Wife's Domicile Is That of Her Husband?

The rule originates in the concept of the unity of husband and wife. One would think that the nineteenth-century legislation that accorded married women a legal existence independent of their husbands would have abolished it. Many courts and legislatures have limited its application and allow married women to establish their own domiciles, but not in all states and not for all purposes.

What Are the Purposes for Which a Married Woman May Establish Her Own Domicile?

First, in all states, a married woman may establish her own domicile if she has grounds for separation or divorce. Second, a married woman may establish her own domicile to satisfy the federal court requirement for diversity jurisdiction.[2] For example, Roseanne was injured while she was a student at a Michigan college. A few years later, when she was married and living in Ohio, she sued the college. Four weeks before she filed suit, her husband moved to Michigan to take a job. Roseanne stayed in Ohio to finish the semester at the school where she was teaching. In order to be able to sue in the Michigan federal court, Roseanne had to be domiciled in a state other than Michigan. When her husband moved to Michigan, did Roseanne become domiciled in Michigan? The court said no, a married woman can have a domicile separate from her husband for purposes of diversity jurisdiction.[3]

In sixteen states and Washington, D.C., a married woman may maintain a separate domicile with her husband's consent or acquiescence.[4] Therefore if Linda went to medical school in Kentucky, with Michael's consent, Kentucky would probably recognize her as domiciled in Kentucky. It is a good idea to get the husband's consent in writing because if a case arises, it will be good evidence. Acquiescence would exist if the husband tolerated his wife's absence for a substantial period of time and made no protestations, or if he abandoned her (in effect, his abandonment would give her cause to establish a separate domicile because she would have grounds for divorce or separation). In twelve states, a married woman may have a separate domicile for purposes of voting;[5] in five, for purposes of jury duty;[6] in six, for purposes of holding public office;[7] in five, for probate;[8] and in six, for purposes of taxation.[9]

Are There Any States in Which a Married Woman May Establish Her Own Domicile for All Purposes?

Yes. She may do so in Alaska and Arkansas.[10] She may also do so in the states that have enacted equal rights amendments (ERA's). (See Chapter 10, page 167, note 3.)

What Is the Effect of Equal Rights Amendments on the Principle that a Married Woman's Domicile Is That of Her Husband?

This principle would clearly be unconstitutional under the state equal rights amendments (and the federal ERA, if it is enacted) as gender-based discrimination. So a married woman is on strong ground if she attempts to establish her own domicile in any of the ERA states, although no cases construing the ERA's on this issue have yet been decided.[11]

NOTES

1. For example, when Linda applies for tuition, the authorities may ask where she has voted, paid taxes, and lived for the past several years, in order to determine whether she is, in fact, domiciled in Kansas. "Domicile" is a confusing concept because the determination of whether someone may have certain privileges is based on the person's past exercise of privileges accorded people domiciled in that state.

2. To decide a case, a court must, among other things, have jurisdiction over the subject matter of the lawsuit. This is obtained by a federal court in two ways: either the issue must be one of federal law or the parties to the suit must be domiciled in different states. The latter is called diversity jurisdiction.

3. *Napletana* v. *Hillsdale College,* 385 F.2d 871 (6th Cir. 1967).

4. Arizona, Arkansas, Delaware, Georgia, Indiana, Kentucky, Missouri, Nevada, New Hampshire, New Jersey, New York, Ohio, Oregon, South Carolina, Tennessee, West Virginia. President's Commission on the Status of Women, *Report of the Committee on Civil and Political Rights* (Washington, D.C., 1963), Table 2, "State Laws Governing Domicile of Married Women," p. 21. This list does not include states that have enacted ERA's.

5. Arizona, California, Kentucky, Maine, Michigan, Nevada, New Jersey, New York, North Carolina, Ohio, Vermont, Wisconsin. *Ibid.*

6. Maine, Nevada, New Jersey, New York, Wisconsin. *Ibid.*

8. Florida, Nevada, New Jersey, New York, North Carolina. *Ibid.*

9. Alabama, Maine, Nevada, New Jersey, New York, South Carolina. *Ibid.*

10. Alaska Statutes Annotated, § 25.15.110 (1962); Arkansas Statutes Annotated, § 34–1307–1309 (1962).

11. See Barbara Brown et al., "The Equal Rights Amendment: A Constiutional Basis for Equal Rights for Women," *Yale Law Journal* 80 (1971), pp. 871, 941, for a comprehensive discussion.

12 / Criminal Law

Besides being considered a crime in twenty states, living together has other consequences within the criminal law. (See Chapter 2.) It can be the basis for the abrogation of parole; it can preclude a conviction for rape; it can lead to criminal prosecution under the "White Slave Trade" Act. Your marital status also affects the likelihood that police will intervene in your disputes; what courts will resolve your disputes; and your liability for crimes other than cohabitation, such as conspiracy and assault.

Keep in mind that the criminal law concerns itself with the punishment of offenses against society, whereas the civil law attempts to remedy offenses against individuals. The criminal law is the main means by which our society vents its moral outrage. The fact that marital status is of relevance in the criminal law demonstrates that living together, sexual relations, and marriage are viewed as moral issues of societal importance. Although you may think the law has no business governing your relationship, it does so in spite of your wishes.

How Will the Fact that You Are Living with Someone Affect Your Chances of Getting or Keeping Probation or Parole?

Simply this: living together may be grounds for denial or revocation of probation or revocation of parole. In addition, a person on probation or parole must obtain permission from his/her supervising officer in order to marry. But let's backtrack a few steps. What are parole and probation?

When a person is convicted of a crime, he/she is either sentenced to prison or put on probation. If put on probation, he/she will spend a designated number of years under the supervision of a probation officer. If a person is sent to prison, he/she will usually be given an "indeterminate sentence." In other words, the minimum and maximum number of years to be served will be specified—e.g., a sentence of from two to ten years. After the two years, the person will be considered for parole. This means that his/her record will be reviewed to determine whether he/she should be released from prison. If the prisoner is released, he/she will be under the supervision of a parole officer and a set of rules. If the parolee violates any of these rules, he/she will be sent back to prison.

Probation and parole are, supposedly, techniques for rehabilitating the criminal. The decision whether a person gets probation or parole hinges not only on the nature of the crime committed but also on an evaluation of his/her chances of "rehabilitation" in a nonprison environment. "Rehabilitation" is a value-laden term. It implies a restoration of the individual to practicing the dominant values of the society. One of the most dominant is the importance of the family. If a person has a closely knit family, his/her chances of getting parole or probation are high. They increase if he/she has roots in a community, has a job, is a churchgoer, wears a suit and tie, supports his/her children, and so on.

It is useful to have a family, but it also must be the right kind of family—a legal family. Corrections departments place a lot of store on form. Convicts have to toe the line even more than the average citizen. They have to be on their best behavior; they have to demonstrate that they are no longer a threat to society.

The way they must do this is by acting according to the book. It was not long ago that New York's book, the *General Rules Governing Parole,* said no living together. Before that, the book said no non-marital or extramarital sexual relations. The constitutionality of these rules was never tested. They appear to be a serious invasion of the parolee's right to privacy. Some states may still have rules like the ones New York has abolished.

As of December 1975, Rule 8 of the *General Rules Governing Parole* says, "I will consult with my parole officer before applying for a license to marry."

The rules used to say that the parolee must obtain written permission from his parole officer before applying for a marriage license. The change seems to indicate that the parole officer may act as the parolee's adviser but lacks authority to say yes or no to marriage. However, the *New York State Parole Officer's Field Manual* has not been updated. It still says, "Granting permission for marriage is one of the most important case decisions. It is the intent of the law that marriage be a permanent institution. The parole officer should give careful and unhurried consideration to each request."[1] If the parole officer still has the power to grant or withhold permission to marry, he/she probably should not have this power. Such authority would appear to conflict with the parolee's constitutional right to marry. In addition, it is questionable that it is the intent of the law that marriage be a permanent institution in light of the increasing ease of divorce.

Nevertheless, you should be aware that there may be similar rules affecting the parolee's rights to marry, to cohabit outside of marriage, and to have sexual intercourse in your state.

Can a Husband Be Convicted for Raping His Wife?

No. It is a legal impossibility for a husband to rape his wife, although it is a physical possibility. The rationale behind this fiction is that the wife is deemed to have given her consent to all sexual relations with her husband by virtue of marriage, and that this applies up to the date of the final divorce decree. So even if husband and wife are separated, he will not be convicted of rape. The fact that rape between husband and wife is a legal impossibility is one indication that the rape laws are designed not to protect women but rather to protect men's interests in certain women. Marriage becomes a license to rape. If the rape laws were really designed to protect the integrity of a woman's body, no such fiction regarding husband and wife would be posited.

Can a Man Be Convicted of Raping a Woman with Whom He Lives?

Oregon and Maine say no.[2] In the other states, it is not a legal impossibility for a man to be convicted of raping a woman he lives with. But it is very unlikely. Why? The answer lies in an understanding of the elements of the crime of rape. There are two kinds of rape—common-law rape and statutory rape. Common-law rape is intercourse accomplished without the woman's consent. Statutory rape is intercourse with a female under an age designated by state law, ranging between ten and twenty-one, with or without her consent.

The major element of the crime of common-law rape is the lack of consent. What kind of evidence indicates lack of consent? The courts hold almost universally that a woman's prior sexual experience is relevant to whether or not she consented to the act in question. In other words, if she had intercourse before, she is likely to have it again and, therefore, she is likely to have consented this time. In the eyes of the courts, the probability of her having consented this time is even greater if she previously had intercourse with the man she now accuses of raping her. So, if the man you are living with rapes you, you will have a very difficult time proving it. You would be better off making a criminal complaint for assault, where your "chasity" would not be in issue, rather than a complaint for rape, where your "chastity" will be dragged all over the courtroom.

You may wonder what chastity has to do with whether you were raped at any given time. The judge in a 1945 case in which a woman who had lived with a man was accusing another man of rape, put it this way: "we hold that evidence of particular acts of immorality with other men shortly before the alleged rape is competent upon the idea that if she has made merchandise of her virtue, that fact will strongly militate against the probability that she did not consent in the case at hand."[3] He doesn't really say why there is a connection between prior chastity and consent, but he gives some indication in his use of the words "made merchandise of her virtue." In the eyes of the law, an unmarried woman is either a virgin or a whore. For male judges and legislators, virginity is *the* important fact. Once a woman is no longer a virgin, why should she refuse intercourse? And if she is no longer virtuous, why should she be protected by the law? This reasoning again demonstrates that rape laws are designed to protect not women but rather the interests men have in women—in this case, in their chastity.

On the other hand, some judges have taken the position that a woman's chastity is irrelevant to whether she consented in a specific case. Unfortunately, however, most of these judges do so in dissenting opinions, which means that their reasoning is not followed. In a 1953 case that overturned the defendant's conviction for rape, the dissenting judge wrote, "Even an immoral woman has some freedom of selection and consent obtained from such a woman by a stunning blow on the jaw is no consent at all."[4]

The question of chastity is raised not only regarding consent but also regarding the credibility of the woman who alleges she was raped. Presumably this is based on the same reasoning: a woman who has had intercourse once is not likely to refuse it again; therefore, if she says she said no, she is probably lying. In that same 1953 rape case, the defendant, Mr. Packineau, and another fellow went out driving with Ms. Loretta Bear and another woman. Ms. Bear accused Mr. Packineau of rape. He dug up some evidence to the effect that she and another man had "cohabitated together as man and wife, slept together in the same bed in the same room during that period of five or more days while picking potatoes." The appeals court said this was relevant to her credibility as a witness:

> To an ordinary person called on to make an appraisal of Loretta's accusation that one of the young men with whom she was out for dalliance on this night had raped her, the reaction would certainly be very different if it were known that she had been openly cohabiting with a young man only a few months before than it would be if she were the unsophisticated young lady she appeared to be.[5]

These cases are more than twenty years old. Presumably, attitudes have changed since then, yet not so the law. It is a rare judge who feels that a woman's sexual history has no bearing on her consent at a given time or on her credibility.[6] That that attitude persists at a time when the incidence of intercourse among college women is high and the incidence among teen-agers is growing is fantastic.[7] It can only be described as wishful thinking.

If the woman is under the age designated in the state law defining statutory rape, the man is in trouble and ignorance of her age is no excuse. In such a case, consent is irrelevant—the female under the statutory age is deemed to be incapable intellectually and emotionally, and therefore legally, of consenting to intercourse. This results in a sort of absolute liability for the man. The female's prior sexual history is generally considered relevant to her credibility, but sympathies tend to lie with her.

The statutory rape rule has come under attack recently both from young feminists who feel that the protection of the state is unjustified and from at least one court speaking on behalf of the accused rapist. In that case, the accused argued that he did not know that the young woman with whom he had intercourse (in which she voluntarily participated) was underage. The lower court said ignorance was no excuse. But the higher court decided that lack of knowledge of her age was a valid defense and over-turned his conviction. The court explained that the presumption that a woman under the statutory age could not consent was unjustified:

> the law makes a conclusive presumption of the lack [of consent] because she is presumed too innocent and naive to understand the implications and nature of her act. . . . The law's concern with her capacity to consent is explained in part by a popular con-ception of the social, moral or personal values which are preserved by the abstinence from sexual indul-gence on the part of a young woman. An unwise disposition of her sexual favor is deemed to do harm both to herself and the social mores by which the community's conduct patterns are established . . . [but] the assumption that age alone will bring an understanding of the sexual act to a young woman is of doubtful validity.[8]

Certainly, protection of young girls is desirable. Statutory rape laws are questionable primarily when the age is set on the high side, between eighteen and twenty-one. Contemporary sexual mores would seem to indicate that the age of consent should be lower. The law concerning rape should be changed to reflect current sexual behavior. A woman's sexual history has nothing to do with whether she was raped *this* time. Social policy does not require that people of college age be protected by statutory rape laws.

Are There Any Criminal Statutes (Other than Those Prohibiting Cohabitation and Fornication) That May Affect You if You Are Living with Someone?

Yes. There is a federal law known as the White Slave Traffic Act, or Mann Act, that makes it a crime to (1) transport a woman or girl in interstate or foreign commerce for the purpose of "prostitution or debauchery, or for any other immoral purpose" or (2) to persuade, induce, entice, or coerce a woman or girl to go from one place to another in interstate or foreign commerce for purposes of prostitution or debauchery or any other immoral purpose, with or without her consent. These provisions carry penalties of a $5,000 fine, up to five years in jail, or both. The Mann Act also makes it a crime to persuade, induce, entice, or coerce a woman or girl under eighteen to travel in interstate or foreign commerce for purposes of prostitution, debauchery, or any other immoral purpose. The penalty is a $10,000 fine, ten years in prison, or both.[9] These provisions were enacted in 1910 to prevent prostitution, on the heels of worldwide concern about the spread of venereal disease. But they have been held to apply to noncommercial sex as well as prostitution via the words "any other immoral purpose." In 1916, the Supreme Court upheld the conviction of a man for violation of the Mann Act where the woman he transported was to become his mistress. There was no profit or commercial motive involved. The Court said:

> The prostitute may, in the popular sense be more degraded in character than the concubine, but the latter none the less must be held to lead an immoral life, if any regard whatever be had to the views that are almost universally held in this country as to the relations which may rightfully, from the standpoint of morality, exist between man and woman in the matter of sexual intercourse.[10]

The decision has not been overruled. That means that if you live in New York and you and your friend decide to go to Cape Cod for a vacation where you will be renting a room together, you can be prosecuted under the Mann Act. The "you," by the way, can be either the man or the woman. The woman transported can be considered an accomplice. However, a woman cannot be charged under the Mann Act for transporting a man for immoral purposes. That has been challenged as being sex discriminatory and, therefore, in violation of the Fifth Amendment. But in *United States* v. *Caesar* a federal district court upheld its constitutionality on the grounds that either a man or a woman can be *charged* with the offense, even though only women can be the subject of the offense.[11] This is a curious decision because if the purpose of the law is to prevent prostitution, it should prevent prostitution of men as well as women. Perhaps in 1910 male prostitution was not a problem; today it might well be considered one. Had it been female or male *prostitutes* and not "transporters" raising the issue of sex discrimination, the case might have gone the other way.

The *Caesar* case involved the transportation of

women to Vietnam allegedly for purposes of prostitution. The defendants also challenged the act on the ground that it unduly restricted their right to privacy in sexual and moral matters in violation of the Ninth Amendment. But the court rejected that argument and said that the Ninth Amendment and case law construing it applied to privacy in the home and marital privacy—not to prostitution. The privacy argument, however, would seem to be valid in cases of private, noncommercial sexual activity between consenting adults, although it has not yet been recognized by a court. Until such a case arises, the Mann Act still lives. It is unlikely that you will be prosecuted for taking a vacation together. But you could be.

Will Police Respond to a Call regarding a Violent Dispute between You and the Person You Are Living with? Will They if You Are Married?

In theory, the relationship between victim and assailant is not supposed to affect a person's right to police protection. In practice, it does. Although more than one eighth of all murders in the United States involve a spouse killing a spouse, police are reluctant to interfere in disputes between people who are married to each other.[12] Police are more willing, however, to interfere in disputes involving people who are just living together. A description of one California woman's experience dramatizes this paradox:

> The woman had known her husband for some time before she married him. When he became violent then, she would call the police and have him put

out of the apartment. But she had children by him and was pressured into marriage for the children's sake. Now, when she calls the police, though it is still her apartment and she pays the rent, the most the police will do is escort her from her home.[13]

The attitude underlying this practice is that marriage gives people the right to treat each other with violence, whereas no such license exists if you are living together. Here, subjective views of marriage are paramount. If the policeman thinks a husband has the right to discipline his wife, then he may consider wife-beating not a crime and therefore none of his business.

If You Have a Violent Dispute While You Are Living Together, Will the Matter Be Handled in Criminal or Family Court? What if You Are Married?

Let's say James gets drunk and slashes Paula with a kitchen knife. In most states, he could be prosecuted for the crime of "assault." In most states, whether Paula and James are married or not, the matter is handled by the criminal-court system. In some states, like New York, if Paula and James were married, the matter would be handled by family court.[14] What is the difference? The main difference is that family court has a wide range of remedies it can use, whereas criminal court can only seek revenge and punish. Family court can make efforts to conciliate the couple; give orders for financial support or protection, visitation, custody; specify conduct of the family members; order medical, psychiatric, or casework treatment. Criminal court can only throw the offender in jail or put him/her on probation.

Where the option of family court is available, the question arises whether couples who are living together are considered a family eligible for its services. In New York, the answer is no. In the decisive case, a man was convicted in criminal court of assault for stabbing the woman he had lived with for eleven years. He appealed, arguing that the case should have been heard in family court because the assault grew out of an intimate family relationship between parties occupying the same household. But the court said that family court had jurisdiction only where there was a legal interdependence between the parties, because the objective of the statute was to preserve a family unit that is consistent with the law and policy of the state—valid ceremonial or common-law marriages.[15] So if you are living together, you cannot go to family court with your disputes. You can seek a restraining order in civil court, but you have available to you none of the services offered to married people by family court.

Can a Husband Be Held Liable for a Crime Committed by His Wife or Vice Versa? What if You Are Living Together?

Whether you are married or unmarried, you cannot be held liable for your partner's crimes. It is a fundamental principle of criminal law that an individual can be held liable only for his/her own acts. (There are some exceptions in corporate and tax laws.)

The only ambiguity in this area affects married

people. Formerly, a husband and wife could not be prosecuted for conspiracy on the theory that they were *one* and it takes *two* to conspire. But now courts are acknowledging that husband and wife are two separate individuals and therefore can conspire to commit a crime: "The fictional unity of husband and wife has been substantially vitiated by the overwhelming evidence that one plus one adds up to two, even in twogetherness [*sic*]."[16]

Similarly, it used to be the case that a husband could not be convicted for stealing the separate property of his wife. Now, however, it is a generally recognized possibility.[17]

NOTES

1. *New York State Parole Officer's Field Manual,* § 206.01, "Case Decisions, Marriage," p. 1.

2. Oregon Revised Statutes, § 163.335 (1953); Maine Revised Statutes Annotated, Title 17A, §§ 252, 253 (West 1964).

3. *Grigsby* v. *Commonwealth of Kentucky,* 299 Ky. 721, 187 S.W.2d 259 (1945).

4. *Packineau* v. *United States,* 202 F.2d 681, 689 (8th Cir. 1953).

5. *Ibid,* pp. 685–686.

6. New York State now has a law that is designed to ensure that it is the defendant, not the victim, who is on trial. Criminal Procedure Law, Section 60.42, effective September 1, 1975, provides that evidence

of a victim's sexual conduct shall not be admissible in a prosecution for rape unless, among other limited exceptions, it proves (1) specific instances of her prior sexual conduct with the accused or (2) that she has been convicted of prostitution.

7. See Arthur M. Vener and Cyrus S. Stewart, "Adolescent Sexual Behavior in Middle America Revisited: 1970–73," *Journal of Marriage and the Family* 36 (1974), pp. 728, 732. The authors studied the sexual activity of approximately 1,900 thirteen-to-seventeen-year-old students from a white, nonmetropolitan upper-working- to upper-middle-class community in Michigan from 1970 to 1973. They found that whereas in 1970, 16.1 percent of the girls had "gone all the way" (had had coitus at least once) in 1973, 22.4 percent had done so.

8. *People* v. *Hernandez*, 39 Cal. Rptr. 361, 393 P.2d 673 (1964).

9. 18 U.S.C. §§ 2421–2423.

10. *Caminetti* v. *United States*, 242 U.S. 470 (1916).

11. *United States* v. *Caesar*, 368 F. Supp. 328 (Wisc. 1973).

12. U.S. Department of Justice, Federal Bureau of Investigation, U.S. Department of Justice Uniform Crime Reports, *Crime in the U.S., 1973* (Washington, D.C., 1974), pp. 9–10. The FBI report also indicates that the wife was the victim in 52 percent of the cases; 49 percent of the victims were black, 50 percent white, and 1 percent of other races.

13. Elizabeth Truninger, "Marital Violence," *Hastings Law Journal* 23 (1974), pp. 259, 272.

14. Under N.Y.S. Family Court Act, Section 812, the family court has original jurisdiction over intrafamily assaults. But it can be waived and the matter will then be handled by the criminal court.

15. *People* v. *Allen,* 27 N.Y.2d 108, 313 N.Y.S.2d 719, 261 N.E.2d 637 (1970).

16. *People* v. *Pierce,* 61 Cal. 2d 879 (1964).

17. *People* v. *Morton,* 308 N.Y. 96, 123 N.E.2d 790 (1954).

13 / The Right Not to Testify

In the autumn of 1975, a woman went on trial on charges of conspiracy and bombing as part of her alleged political activities in the 1960's. Several years earlier, she and a man had lived together. The prosecutor subpoenaed him to testify to whatever he knew about her. He refused to testify, and was held in contempt and sentenced to jail for the duration of the trial; he was also threatened with being charged with criminal contempt, for which he could serve a much longer sentence. If they had been married, he could not have been forced to testify on pain of contempt, because confidential communications between husband and wife are considered privileged.

*Can You Be Required to Testify before a Court
or Grand Jury to Communications You Have
Had with the Person You Are Living With?*

As the preceding case shows, the answer is yes. Of course, it is important to realize that being required to testify does not mean that you will be tortured into testifying. It means that you can be held in contempt of court and thrown in jail if you refuse to do so. While you must pay for your silence, at least you may preserve it.

In contrast, if you were married you could not be thrown in jail for refusing to testify to confidential communications you had with your husband or wife. A communication is considered confidential if it would not have been made but for the relationship— e.g., your wife tells you she murdered someone, or your husband tells you he is not reporting all his income to the IRS; you probably would not have been a sounding board if you hadn't been on intimate terms.

The theory behind the privilege is that confidences lie at the heart of the relationship between husband and wife. Society's interest in knowing the substance of these communications is outweighed by its interest in protecting and strengthening the relationship.

Why are people who are married and those who are living together treated differently? Certainly people who are living together exchange confidences. Why should they be denied the "husband-wife" privilege? The argument against extending the privilege is that its purpose is to bolster *marriage*, not living together. Our law, in fact, disapproves of and criminalizes cohabitation. On the other hand, the purpose of the privilege is not to protect marriage per se, but the relationship between men and women that has historically been designated marriage. In contemporary society, where formal marriage is often transient and where living together is increasingly accepted, the terms "husband" and "wife" are not broad enough to effect that purpose. The extension of confidentiality to people who are living together would serve the basic intent of the privilege in our present social context. Failure to extend it may also violate the zone of privacy accorded people who are living together that was acknowledged in *Eisenstadt v. Baird*. (See page 41.)

These and other arguments were raised unsuccessfully. But they should certainly be made again. This is one area in which people who are married and those who are living together should be treated alike because the societal interest in promoting stability by encouraging relationships of trust is at stake in either case.

14 / Public Benefits

Last Saturday, Jane called her grandmother in Florida. An elderly male voice answered the phone. "Who's this and what are you doing answering my grandmother's telephone?" Jane demands. "This is George and it's my phone too!" he responds. It is the younger generation's turn to be taken aback. Has Jane's grandmother thrown her scruples to the wind? Has she lost her senses? Or does her relationship have an economic motive?

The young have no monopoly on living together. Elderly couples who receive social security may often find it to their financial advantage to live together and remain unmarried. Is that what is meant by legislating morality?

Bill and Ellen wake up one day and discover they are sixty-five. Both have worked for the twenty-five years of their marriage—but Bill has earned three times as much as Ellen. Both have paid the social security tax. They trot down to their local social security office to find out what rewards await them for enjoyment in their golden years. Ellen learns an adage she'd never heard before: "You are a worker when you contribute, but a wife when you collect." Translation: the wife who works outside the home pays the same amount of social security tax as any worker with the same salary; yet, on retirement, she receives either one-half her husband's stipend or a stipend based on her own wage level, whichever is larger. Since women tend to earn less than men, odds are her stipend will be less than one-half his or very little more than that. If the stipend computed on the basis of her own earnings is less than one-half his, she will receive social security benefits based on his earnings, not her own. Ironically, even if she had never earned any money or paid any social security taxes, she would get the same benefit. If the stipend computed on the basis of her own earnings is more than half her husband's stipend, it is probably not very much more. Are the few dolars more per month sufficient for twenty-five years of nine-to-five (not to mention five-to-twelve when she did the housework)? The problem for the wife who works outside the home is that her social security contributions are gratuitous—she would get the same or nearly the same benefits even if she had never earned a cent. This looks like the same reinforcement of the stay-at-home wife we saw in the tax laws.

These are just two examples of how your marital status affects your eligibility for public benefits. Public benefits are benefits that flow from the government or by virtue of its mandate. They include social security, medicare, food stamps, welfare, veterans' benefits, workmen's and unemployment compensation. Since public benefits are a vital part of survival in our world, you would do well to take them into consideration in deciding to marry or to live together.

What Is Social Security and What Kinds of Benefits Are Available?

Social security is basically a mandatory insurance policy. You rarely get out what you put in, but that's the risk you take for getting anything at all.

Social security offers four kinds of benefits: (1) retirement—commonly called "old-age"—benefits, (2) survivor's benefits, (3) disability benefits, and (4) lump-sum death benefits.

The retirement benefit is what most people think of when they think of social security. To receive it you must have worked for 6¼ years (if you reach sixty-two in 1976, and longer if you reach sixty-two in subsequent years) in a job in which you have paid social security taxes and you must have reached the age of sixty-two, although if you wait until sixty-five your benefits will be higher. The tax is paid by the employee (it's the Federal Insurance Contribution Amount, or FICA, deduction from your paycheck) and matched by the employer. As of 1976, 5.85 percent of your salary goes to social security. If you are self-employed, the rate is 9.7 percent. Whether you earn $5,000 or $15,300 per year, you pay 5.85 percent. But if you earn over $15,300 per year, you pay no more than 5.85 percent of $15,300, or $893 per year. Thus the tax structure is regressive—the rate decreases as income increases (over $15,300).

The amount of your retirement stipend is determined on the basis of your average annual salary. But you cannot get more than $364.00 per month if you reach 65 in 1976, or $291.20 per month if you reach 62 in 1976; you cannot get less than $101.40 if you reach 65 in 1976, or less than $81.20

if you reach 62 in 1976 (assuming you have contributed and worked for the required number of years).

Almost all workers contribute to social security except employees of the federal government, farmworkers, and people who do not work for pay, such as homemakers.

When a male worker retires, his wife is also entitled to a stipend of up to half his stipend. When a female worker retires, her husband is entitled to a stipend of up to half hers, but only if he was her dependent—i.e., only if she contributed over half his support. In other words, the law presumes the wife to be dependent, even though she might not be; it presumes the husband not to be dependent, even though he might well be. Thus if Mary was a dental hygienist and was covered by social security but her husband Paul was a farmworker and was not covered by social security, he could get no social security on the basis of her earnings unless he could demonstrate that he was her dependent. In contrast, if Mary was the farmworker and earned three times as much as Paul, whose job had social security coverage, she would automatically be entitled to social security benefits based on his earnings, despite the fact that he may have been dependent on her! This is double-edged sex discrimination.

A divorced wife or widow can collect social security on the basis of her husband's earnings only if they were married for twenty years and she has not remarried. The only exception is that a divorced woman may receive survivors' benefits for a child from the marriage left in her care.[1] A divorced husband gets nothing on the basis of his former wife's earnings unless he can show he was financially de

pendent on her and has not remarried. These provisions leave a lot of people uncovered—divorced
women who were married for less than twenty years
who have never worked outside the home. They
reflect sex bias, as well—the divorced husband of
twenty years gets nothing on his wife's earnings
unless he can prove dependency, while his ex-wife
gets coverage whether she was dependent on him
or not.

The survivors' benefits are benefits paid to the
surviving spouse of a covered worker (male/female)
if he/she has reached sixty or sixty-two, to the
widow/widower of any age who is left with a child
(these, oddly enough, are called "mother's benefits"), to any surviving children, or to dependent
parents.

Disability benefits are payments made to the
worker who becomes so disabled before sixty-five
that he/she can no longer work. The worker must
have worked for a specified number of years in a
job where he/she paid the social security tax, of
course.

Lump-sum death payments are payments made on
a covered worker's death to his/her surviving spouse.
In 1976, it is $255.

*Why Is It Sometimes to the Advantage of People
Now on Social Security to Live Together Rather
than Get Married?*

An older couple, both of whom receive social security, can often receive higher benefits if the woman
continues being somebody else's widow than if they

marry. For example, Mrs. Elizabeth Shaw receives $364 per month as the surviving widow of Mr. Shaw, who earned the maximum amount covered by social security all his life.[2] Mr. George Burke receives $364 per month as a retired worker who earned as much as Mr. Shaw. Their combined income from social security would be $728. If they married, however, Mrs. Shaw would receive benefits as Mr. Burke's wife, no longer as Mr. Shaw's widow. Together they would receive one and one-half times Mr. Burke's stipend, $546, which is $182 per month *less* than if they merely lived together. No bargain there. The reason for the difference is that a wife is thought to need less than a widow; it's the old two-can-live-almost-as-cheaply-as-one syndrome, which, to some extent, is valid—one rent, one automobile, and so on. But prices being what they are, neither stipend is really adequate, and people will take as much as they can get.

It is also financially more expedient to live together if Mr. Shaw had a higher salary than Mr. Burke, since benefits are tied to income (but there is a minimum and maximum benefit regardless of income).

The anomaly could be remedied by avoiding a derivative benefit system. As it stands, Mrs. Shaw, who kept house all her married life but made no money and no social security contributions, *derives* her right to benefits from her husband's contributions; therefore the amount she receives is dependent on how much *he* earned. If her labor as a homemaker were given a value on which she paid social security taxes or which was given a social security credit (more about this later), her benefits would not have to be derivative. In that way, there would be no particular benefit or detriment associated with marital status.

Gearing the social security system to individuals rather than to relationships raises the issue of who pays for the homemaker's coverage. The problem with requiring homemakers to pay a social security tax is that they generally are in a nonliquid position —they earn no money out of which to pay tax. A credit system is preferable and there is ample precedent for it. In the military, for example, a person's social security coverage is paid for by the government. Members of religious orders who take vows of poverty and who receive no monetary payment have their social security coverage paid for by the order to which they belong. Similar credits for homemakers should be paid for out of income tax or FICA revenues. Women now get money as widows that they could get equally well as homemakers, only it would then travel with them, rather than cease with their remarriage.

If You Are Living Together, Can You Receive Social Security Benefits Based on Each Other's Contributions?

No. Social security is a family affair. You have to be either ceremonially married or demonstrate a valid common-law marriage to be entitled to receive benefits deriving from another. Furthermore, if you believe you are married and it turns out that your husband is still legally married to someone else, *she*, not you, gets his social security benefits. Odd? It happens.

Is there any way to get around the requirement

of a valid marriage? No. You cannot assign your social security benefits (before you receive them), nor can you bequeath them by will. When you die, they stop. You cannot even seriously get around the marriage requirement by one of you adopting the other. Benefits for a child only last until he/she is eighteen, or twenty-two if a full-time student.

But, you say, if my relationship in fact resembles that of any married couple, why shouldn't we be entitled to the benefits. Probably the best answer is administrative—nonceremonial marriages are hard to prove. But, you say, people with valid common-law marriages are allowed to try to prove theirs. The response to that is that the Social Security Administration doesn't like them either. The states have phased out common-law marriage precisely because of the difficulty in ascertaining who is married to whom for purposes of allocation of benefits.

The broadest remedy for this inequity is to eliminate the derivative benefit system for spouses rather than to extend it to people who are living together. The derivative benefit system for spouses is premised on the idea that one supports the other—that one person, usually the wife, is not part of the labor force. If her work were valued enough in its own right for the government to provide her with social security credits, the need for derivative benefits would cease. Homemakers should be treated as *workers* for purposes of social security, not as wives. That doesn't mean that the homemaker-wife would lose anything; it means only that her benefits would be based on the value of her own labor, not the value of her husband's. If these derivative benefits are eliminated, then people just living together will have no cause to envy their married counterparts.

What Are Some of the Other Inequities in the Present Social Security System?

The greatest inequity is that the benefits are not large enough. But beyond that, like the income tax laws, the social security system in some respects favors (1) the married person and (2) the arrangement where the husband works for money and the wife works for free—i.e., in the home.

How Does the Social Security System Disadvantage the Single Person with a Dependent Partner?

Take, for example, Sam and Jim. They are both sixty-five; they had the same average annual salary and they paid the same amount of social security taxes. Sam supported the woman he lived with; Jim supported his wife. Yet Sam will get less than Jim and his wife in social security. Why? Because of the derivative spousal benefit.

How Does the Social Security System Reinforce the Traditional Division of Labor within the Family?

An assumption implicit in the Social Security Act is that the husband is the breadwinner and the wife is the homemaker. When a man retires, he gets x amount and his wife gets $\frac{1}{2}x$ amount automatically. When a woman retires, she gets y amount. But her husband does not get $\frac{1}{2}y$ amount unless he can show that she contributed over half his support. In other words, she is presumed to be supported by him even if she is not; he is presumed not to be supported by her even if he is.

The same idea operates with survivors' benefits. If a husband who has contributed to social security dies, his wife automatically gets survivors' benefits; if a wife who has contributed to social security dies, her husband must prove he was supported by her to collect survivors' benefits. A retired man, Leon Goldfarb, of Jamaica, Queens, successfully challenged this presumption in the Federal District Court for the Eastern District of New York. Mr. Goldfarb had been a managing analyst for the U.S. Signal Corps until 1971, when he retired at age sixty-seven. As a federal employee, he had paid no social security taxes. His wife had been a secretary in the New York City public school system for twenty-five years and had paid social security taxes. When his wife died in 1968, Mr. Goldfarb applied for survivors' benefits. But his application was denied because he could not prove that his wife had contributed over one-half his support. He sued the Social Security Administration on grounds that the statute discriminated on the basis of sex. If he had been the secretary and she had been the managing analyst and he had died, she would have been entitled to survivors' benefits, no questions asked. The court said that that was sex discrimination and violated equal protection in that it deprived women of the same protection for their families which men receive.[3]

It seems likely that, on appeal, the Supreme Court will uphold the district court's decision in light of its decision in the *Wiesenfeld* case, which will be discussed below.

Until March 19, 1975, the same situation prevailed regarding "mother's benefits." Those are benefits available to the families of workers who die before they reach retirement age. If a man died leaving minor children, his wife would automatically receive benefits. But if a woman died leaving minor children, her husband would receive "mother's benefits" only if he could show that she had contributed over half his support. The purpose behind the law is to permit women who lost their breadwinners to remain home with the children. The assumption is that a man who lost his wife will continue to work even if left with children. Paula Wiesenfeld, a woman in her twenties, worked as a teacher and made social security contributions for several years. Tragically, she died in childbirth. Her husband, Simon, had been a computer programmer, but he quit his job when he was unable to find a competent person to care for their infant, Jacob. Simon applied for survivors' benefits for Jacob and "mother's benefits" for himself. Jacob's claim was accepted, but Simon's was denied on the ground that he had failed to show that Paula had contributed over one half his support. Simon appealed his case to the Supreme Court and won. The Court said, "Given the purpose of enabling the surviving parent to remain at home to care for minor children, the gender-based distinction of 402(g) is entirely irrational."[4] The survivors' (in this case, also known as "mother's") benefits are not large enough to encourage men in Simon's situation to suddenly quit their jobs. But men now have the option of doing so—another step in their liberation from traditional roles. Another important aspect of the *Wiesenfeld* decision is that it recognizes that women who work outside the home have as much right to have their families protected as men. The illusion that men are the sole providers is on its way out.

Is a Woman Who Works outside the Home Better Off Married or Unmarried as Far as Her Social Security Benefits Are Concerned?

For a variety of reasons, the contributions a married woman who works for wages makes to social security tend to be virtually worthless to her as long as she stays married. But if she gets divorced, they become invaluable. Let's examine why.

The wife of a person entitled to social security benefits is entitled to a retirement benefit based on her husband's income as long as her own stipend is less than half her husband's stipend.

Let's say Bill, whose "average annual salary" was $6,000 (nearly the maximum covered by social security) is entitled to a stipend of $344.10 per month.[5] His wife, Ellen, whose "average annual salary" was $4,000 per year, is entitled to a stipend of $262.60 per month. Her stipend is more than one half his, so she receives benefits on her own account. If she had not worked outside the home, she would have received $172.05 per month, one half her husband's basic monthly benefit. What she gets as a retired worker is only $90.55 per month more than what she would get as a wife. Put another way, despite the fact that her contributions entitle her to $262.60 worth of benefits, in effect, she will receive only $90.55 in benefits for all her years of contributions and work—that is, she will receive only $90.55 more for working outside the home then if she had never worked.

If she were unmarried, she would get her $262.60 per month and have done. So she is not better off unmarried. The disparity exists between married women with salaries and married women without salaries. There is little incentive in the social security laws for married women to work.

The one incentive that exists is the provision that a wife who is divorced before twenty years of marriage loses all rights to social security benefits based on her husband's earnings. With today's high divorce rates, many women are affected by this provision. A woman who has earned money all her life will be in a much better financial position should she get divorced than one who has been a homemaker. Until the law permits homemakers to get a social security tax credit for their work in the home, women who are divorced before the twentieth year of their marriage will lack social security coverage. Changing marriage patterns seem to dictate a change in the law to reflect the increasing independence of the partners.

Do the Social Security Laws Penalize Married Couples with More than One Earner in Any Other Way?

Yes. The amount you contribute to social security is not tied to your income at the higher income levels. There is a ceiling: if your income is $15,300 or more, you pay the maximum $895 per year. In effect, the rate structure is regressive—at $15,300, your payments are as high as those of someone earning $100,000 per year, which means that you pay a much higher percentage than he/she does.

How does that affect the two-earner family? Let's say Joe-husband earns $10,000 and Mabel-wife earns $10,000, for a combined income of $20,000 per year. Their social security contributions (computed at the rate of 5.85 percent) come to about $1,170 per year. But if either Joe or Mabel earned $20,000 and the other had no earnings, the social security contributions would come to $895 (the maximum), which is $275 *less*.

If the Person I Live with Gets Injured on the Job, Can I Benefit from Workmen's Compensation?

If a worker is injured or dies on the job, he/she and his/her dependents become entitled to workmen's compensation benefits. "Dependents" is the statutory way of saying relatives. The legislatures don't think dependent nonrelatives should be secured against the injury or death of the person who supports them. Underlying this thinking is the administrative efficiency concern—"if we had to determine if he/she was dependent, we'd be here all day"—and the concern with fraud—"think of all the cheaters." Be that as it may, if you are not married, ceremonially or at common law, you cannot benefit.

If I Live with Someone, Can I or My Children Be Denied Welfare?

In 1968, the Alabama "substitute father" rule that children could be denied Aid to Families with Dependent Children (AFDC) benefits if their mother cohabited with any able-bodied man was invalidated.[6] Since then, states have tried three ways of keeping things clean at home and reducing the welfare roles: (1) by requiring that AFDC recipients cooperate in paternity suits against the fathers of their illegitimate children as a condition of aid, (2) by reducing the stipend if a lodger is present who pays no rent, and (3) by making it a crime for a man to share lodging and meals with a welfare recipient without sharing expenses.[7] What does each mean to you?

The first, requiring that you participate in support or paternity proceedings as a condition of aid, is to get the father to support his child so that welfare doesn't have to. If you are on welfare, living together, and your friend is the father, it should not create much of a problem. He probably won't mind cooperating. However, you will probably feel that your privacy has been invaded. But no court will yet agree with you. The New York statute was challenged as being in conflict with the Social Security Act, which established AFDC. But the Social Security Act was amended to conform to the New York law while the case was being litigated. So although the Supreme Court held that the New York provision *did* conflict with the Social Security Act, the amendment made the decision irrelevant for practical purposes.[8] Now the Social Security Act requires that state AFDC plans require recipients to cooperate in establishing the paternity of children born out of wedlock as a condition of eligibility.[9] Therefore if you wish to stay on welfare, you will have to cooperate in the paternity suit.

The second, requiring a reduction in the shelter allowance of a family receiving AFDC because a "recipient is living with a man to whom she is not married," has been invalidated by the Supreme Court.[10] In an eight-to-one opinion, the judges decided that the requirement conflicted with the Social Security Act, which provides that "the income only of the [legally obligated] parent . . . will be considered available . . . in the absence of proof of actual contributions." That means that your AFDC shelter stipend cannot be reduced because you are living with someone who is not legally obligated to support your children. Note that the court did *not* decide the case on constitutional grounds. It avoids doing this whenever it can. The lower court did address the constitutional issues. It said that the New York statute did not violate freedom of association or the right to privacy, but that it did establish an uncalled-for irrebuttable presumption that the lodger paid to support the children, and that this violated due process. After describing the difficulties Mrs. D, the welfare recipient, faced and the positive function the "lodger" played in the lives of her and her children, the judge perceptively wrote: "The poor do not necessarily cohabit on a bed of roses."[11]

The third, making it a crime to share meals and lodging with a welfare recipient without sharing expenses, is still on the books in at least one state—Oregon. The Oregon statute says: "No male person over the age of 18 years . . . shall habitually accept subsistence or lodging in the dwelling place of any female householder who is the recipient of aid."[12]

Before their marriage, Sandra and Ernest Bearcub were indicted under this statute, he for doing it, she for aiding and abetting. Their convictions, and the statute, were upheld in spite of the apparent sex-discriminatory aspect of the law.[13] In addition, California has a statute making it a misdemeanor to use welfare funds in a manner inconsistent with the best interests of the children on whose behalf the grant is made.[14] So if a person living with the parent does not pay expenses, he/she may be charged with this crime.

How Does the Fact that You Are Living with Someone Affect Your Ability to Get Food Stamps?

The food stamp program is geared to households, not individuals, but you do not have to be related to be eligible; you can get food stamps if you are living together and meet the other eligibility requirements.

That has not always been so. Before June 1973, the Food Stamp Act made ineligible any household whose members were not all related to each other. In June 1973, the Supreme Court invalidated the requirement on the basis that it did not further the purposes of the act—"to safeguard the health and well-being of the Nation's population and raise levels of nutrition among low-income households and . . . to strengthen our agricultural economy."[15]

How Does the Fact that You Are Living with Someone Affect Your Ability to Get Medicaid or Medicare?

It doesn't. Medicare and medicaid do not condition your eligibility for benefits on your relationship to someone. In other words, your right to medicare or medicaid is your own; it does not derive from someone else.

If You Are Living with Someone, Can You Receive His/Her Veterans' Benefits?

All veterans, except those who have been dishonorably discharged, are entitled to receive benefits for service-connected injury they have suffered. Benefits paid as a result of service-connected death are payable to certain beneficiaries—a spouse (valid common-law or ceremonial marriage), a child (unmarried person under eighteen, or twenty-three if a student, who is legitimate, legally adopted, or illegitimate but who has been acknowledged in writing or judicially decreed to be the father's child), or a parent.[16] If you are living together, therefore, you are not entitled to these benefits.

Can You Be Deprived of Your Veterans' Benefits for Living with Someone?

If you are dishonorably discharged from the service, you must forfeit all your veterans' benefits. You can be dishonorably discharged for offenses involving "moral turpitude." (See "Can You Be Dismissed from the Military for Living Together?", page 142.) But if you have not been dishonorably discharged, your veterans' benefits cannot be terminated because you are living with someone.

Can You Get Unemployment Insurance Benefits if the Person You Live with Loses His/Her Job?

A person who involuntarily becomes unemployed is entitled to receive unemployment compensation at a rate and for a length of time that varies state by state. In a few states, dependents are eligible for benefits, too. But as with workmen's compensation, "dependents" means relatives. So if you are living together, you do not qualify.

NOTES

1. When the benefits are for *children,* there is no requirement that the parents be married for twenty years. So a divorced woman with custody of a child whose ex-husband is disabled receives disability benefits on behalf of the child.

2. $3,600 for 1951–1954; $4,200 for 1955–1958; $4,800 for 1959–1965; $6,600 for 1966–1967; $7,800 for 1968–1971; $9,000 for 1972; $10,800 for 1973; $13,200 for 1974; and $14,100 for 1975.

3. *Goldfarb* v. *Secretary of the U.S. Department of Health, Education and Welfare,* 396 F. Supp. 308 (E.D.N.Y. 1975), appeal to U.S. Supreme Court docketed as *Mathews* v. *Goldfarb* February 23, 1976, Docket No. 75–699.

4. *Weinberger* v. *Wiesenfeld,* 420 U.S. 636 (1975).

5. For social security purposes, "average annual salary" is the average not of your *total* salary but of the amount you have earned up to the maximum covered by social security for each given year. See note 2.

6. *King* v. *Smith,* 392 U.S. 309 (1968).

7. Barbara Allen Babcock et al., *Sex Discrimination and the Law: Causes and Remedies* (Boston and Toronto: Little, Brown & Co., 1975), p. 770.

8. *Lascaris* v. *Shirley,* 420 U.S. 730 (1975).

9. Social Security Act, § 402(a), Public Law 93–647, effective July 1, 1975.

10. *Van Lare* v. *Hurley,* 421 U.S. 338 (1975).

11. *Van Lare* v. *Hurley,* 380 F. Supp. 167, 171 (E.D.N.Y. 1974).

12. Oregon Revised Statutes, § 418.140; Babcock et al., *Sex Discrimination,* p. 575, n. 6.

13. *State* v. *Bearcub,* Ore. App., 465 P.2d 252 (1970); Oregon Revised Statutes, § 418.140 (1953); Babcock et al., *Sex Discrimination,* p. 575, n. 6.

14. California Welfare and Institutions Code, § 11480 (West 1972); Babcock et al., *Sex Discrimination,* p. 575, n. 6.

15. *U.S. Department of Agriculture* v. *Moreno,* 413 U.S. 528, 533 (1973).

16. 38 U.S.C. § 101(4).

15 / Private Benefits

Private benefits are all those benefits that do not derive from the government. Basically, we are talking about insurance, credit, and fringe benefits of employment like pensions and health-care or disability plans. What, if any, are your rights?

Can You Be Denied Insurance Coverage for Living with Someone?

At least two women have been denied automobile insurance because they were living with men to whom they were not married. Whether that is legally permissible remains an open question; there are strong arguments that it should not be the basis for denial of coverage.

One woman, a forty-year-old-secretary, moved to Connecticut in 1970. That July, she applied to the Aetna Life Insurance Company for an auto insurance policy, which was granted. She had been driving for eighteen years without an accident or violation of any kind, and she had always been insured. Nevertheless, in October, Aetna refused to renew her policy. Although she made extensive inquiries, she could not find out why. She applied to several other insurance companies but was turned down by all of them. Why? Solely because Aetna had failed to renew her policy. Ultimately, she obtained assigned-risk coverage, the plan by which "uninsurables" are insured, but at higher premiums.

Finally, in May 1971, she was notified by the Retail Credit Company, which had done the credit investigation for Aetna, that the reason her policy had not been renewed was that she was "practically living with her boyfriend." The revelation was prompted by the newly enacted Fair Credit Reporting Act. She brought suit against Aetna, the other insurance companies that had refused to insure her, and Retail Credit. She asserted three grounds: first, that Retail Credit's failure to notify her promptly of the reason her renewal was denied was a violation of the Fair Credit Reporting Act; second, that the investigation into her private life was an unlawful invasion of her privacy; and third, that the insurance companies to which she applied after Aetna conspired to boycott her business and that of others similarly situated without knowing the basis for the nonrenewal of her policy by Aetna, in violation of the antitrust laws. Her case is still pending in the federal district court in Connecticut.

An assistant professor at a prestigious university faced the same problem. She applied to State Farm Insurance Company for automobile insurance coverage in January 1972, and her application was granted. But in mid-February, her policy was canceled. Why? Because "she lived without benefit of wedlock with a member of the opposite sex." She sued State Farm and the Retail Credit Company, which had done the credit investigation for State Farm. However, another company agreed to insure her and at a lower rate, so she could prove no damages. Her case was resolved with a stipulation of dismissal. That means basically that both sides agreed to call the suit a draw. But at least State Farm admitted that the reason it had canceled her policy was that she was living with a man.

These two women are not alone. As a result of the Fair Credit Reporting Act, which enables a person to discover the contents of an investigation of his/her credit-worthiness, more people are finding out why they were rejected for insurance coverage and other types of credit. Sometimes, as here, the grounds bear a questionable relationship to whether a person is a good credit risk.

Why do the insurance companies refuse to insure people who are living with someone? The argument goes like this: people with an unstable life-style are unstable people and, therefore, bad risks. But, in fact, the insurance companies have not shown that there is a connection between living together and being a poor driver. The same thing goes for other types of insurance—do people who live together die earlier than those who are married or who are single and do not live together? Are they more accident prone? Do their homes burn more readily? And so on. Another argument in the automobile insurance area is that there is a great likelihood that the other person will use the insured's car, and therefore the likelihood of accident is greater. The problem with that argument is that it is not applied to any other situation in which the insured's car is likely to be used by others—as in a family. Why should people who are living together be treated any differently from the one-car, two-driver family? If the risk is greater because more people will drive the car, the premiums perhaps should be higher, but insurance should not be denied.

If living together doesn't necessarily make you a bad risk, then what are the real reasons behind the refusal of insurance coverage? The most convincing reason appears to be that insurance companies actually have an interest in denying coverage. It is to their financial advantage to deny people coverage because these "uninsurables" then get put into assigned-risk plans. An assigned-risk plan provides statutorily mandated insurance coverage for "uninsurables" at higher premiums. The insurance companies benefit in two ways: first, assigned-risk categories exact higher premiums, thus more revenue per insured; and second, the more people in the assigned-risk class who are actually decent risks, the lower the accident rate, so the liability of the insurer is reduced. Of course, people who are living together are not the only victims of this incentive to declare people uninsurable—people who have foreign accents, are less than avid housekeepers, residents of "bad" neighborhoods (however defined), and homosexuals are all in the same boat. Their "sin" may have nothing at all to do with their credit-worthiness.

Since no case has been decided on this issue, we do not know where you stand if you are denied insurance because you are living together. Some people encounter no difficulty at all; others do. As more public and legal pressure is put on insurance companies, they may be encouraged to revise their practices. There are several legal legs to stand on. The Fair Credit Reporting Act (FCRA) requires an oral disclosure to the individual concerned of the nature and substance of the file an insurance or credit company maintains on him/her and the identification of the credit-reporting or -investigating agency.[1] This enables you to know something of what you are up against. Until the FCRA, all this was done in utter secret. However, the act does not go far enough in some instances and goes too far in others. An individual does not have the right to *see* the report made on him, so the information he receives orally may be inaccurate or incomplete; he does not have the opportunity to know the sources from which the information about him was obtained, so there is a chance that unreliable information was the basis for his rejection; his permission does not have to be obtained to investigate him, nor does the scope of the investigation have to be revealed. The act goes too far in that it gives credit-reporting companies a partial immunity from suit: they cannot be sued for defamation, negligence, or invasion of privacy unless you can show malice or willful intent to injure.

Despite all the inadequacies of the act, it does require that the credit-reporting or -investigating agencies adopt procedures that consider the confidentiality, accuracy, relevancy, and proper utilization of the information they are gathering. Where the company cannot demonstrate the relevancy of the information sought, as is the case here, it may be found to be in violation of the act.

As in the case against Aetna, an antitrust claim may have possibilities. Invasion of privacy arguments are hard to make successfully here because of the difficulty of showing any action on the part of the state. Finally, if your policy is being canceled because you are living with someone, you may be able to assert breach of contract, which you could not do if you never got a policy in the first place.

Can You Insure the Life of the Person You Live With?

To take out an insurance policy on another person you must have an insurable interest in that person, that is, an interest in that person that the law will recognize. Wives have an insurable interest in their husbands and vice versa; creditors have insurable interests in their debtors. You might have an insurable interest in the person you live with if you were financially dependent on him/her and could persuade an insurance company of this. In addition, you could probably insure the other parent of your minor child based on support or child care furnished even without showing that you were financially dependent.

Is the Person You Live with Covered by Your Insurance Policy?

Some types of insurance policies, like life insurance, enable you to name the beneficiaries. In that case, if you name the person you are living with, he/she will benefit. Similarly, some insurance policies enable you to obtain coverage for specific people. Here too, if you name the person you are living with, he/she will be covered.

The real question arises when you have not named or could not have named the person you are living with as one covered by the policy. Then the language of the policy—the fine print—takes over. For example, Catherine Brown had fire insurance that covered the loss due to fire of personal property in her dwelling belonging to her or any member of her "family." She lived with James Hubbard and their child. When her house was destroyed by fire, James sought compensation for over $1,000 worth of his clothing that had been destroyed in the blaze. The court was called upon to decide whether he was a member of her "family." The court said no: "No case has been called to our attention where a meretricious relationship has been graced by the word 'family,' and the word as used in its most liberal interpretation must have meant persons of the insured's household bearing some kinship to her."[2] This rule seems to be typical of that in other states. So in writing an insurance policy, make sure you name the persons you wish to be covered by it.

Is the Person You Live with a Member of Your Family or Household for Purposes of a "Family-Exclusion Clause" in an Insurance Policy?

A "family-exclusion clause" is a clause found in many types of insurance policies—most often automobile insurance—that precludes recovery for personal injury against the insurance company by a member of the insured's family. The reason for it is to prevent the possibility of collusive suits; in other words, to prevent Mr. and Mrs. A from agreeing that he will crack up the car insured in her name just so he can sue her for injuries he sustained. These clauses read something like this: "This insurance does not apply . . . to bodily injury to the insured or any member of the family of the insured residing in the same household as the insured." So the question, once again, is whether the person you are living with is a member of your family for purposes of this type of clause. Most states say no.[3] That interpretation has the effect of permitting the person you live with to sue you although if he/she were your spouse, he/she could not. Here the courts are caught between two policies: first, that lawsuits that are the product of collusion should be discouraged; and second, that the law will accord status only to ceremonial marriage (except in common-law marriage states). Thus there is nothing to prevent you and the person you are living with from agreeing to have an automobile "accident" so that one of you can collect insurance. It seems that the fear of collusive lawsuits is somewhat unfounded where recovery by family members for personal injury is barred, because few people would deliberately injure themselves to collect insurance. However, the fear is deeply entrenched in the insurance business.

One state court that has held that the person living with the insured was a family member is in a common-law marriage state—South Carolina. Since the woman was considered to be a family member, she came within the family-exclusion clause and could not recover. Ironically, the man she was living with already had a wife, so in effect, the court was allowing him two wives![4] The court may have wanted to find a reason to keep her from recovering. But whatever its motives, it probably adopted the rule that is most relevant to the factual situation, because if collusion is a problem with a married couple, it will also be a problem with unmarried people who share a household.

Will Your Insurance Policy Be Invalidated if You Say You Are Married When You Apply but Are Actually Just Living Together?

This kind of misrepresentation will invalidate the policy only if it is "material." It will be material if the insurer would not have accepted the application had a truthful answer been given. Under that definition, lying about your marital status and living situation would be material because if the insurance company knew you were living with someone, it would probably deny you insurance. The issue arose in a recent Oregon case, however, and the court found that material misrepresentation was not proved. In that case, Donald Bunn purchased life insurance in 1965. On his application he wrote that he was married. Actually, he was just living with Nancy and had been for about fifteen years, during which they had two children. Shortly after the policy was signed, Nancy and Donald were married and Donald left for Vietnam. He died there one year later. When Nancy sued for the life insurance proceeds, the insurance company argued that Donald's misrepresentation that he was married was material and that therefore the policy should be void. But the court said that there was no evidence that the insurance company would have denied him the policy if he had said he was single. Therefore the misrepresentation was not material and Nancy got the insurance proceeds. The testimony of an insurance company officer quoted in the court's opinion is revealing:

> Q. And as an Underwriter, what has marital status to do with life insurance risks, mortality, expectancy and so on?

A. Well, there are several factors involved. The first is that persistency may not be as favorable as on a married person, he might not continue his premiums. There may be other parties involved, and therefore, we think that the mortality rating might be higher; on the married person, it seems to be more stable, and he also seems to be more cautious in his attitude and his way of living.

Q. Are you talking about this from the standpoint of a chance a person takes with accidents or the chance he takes with homicide?

A. It could be chances with homicide or any sort of violence at all, plus the moral risk.

Q. What do you mean by "the moral risk"?

A. If the person is married, we feel that he is a more stable person and that he is more settled than one who is not.

Q. Are these pretty general observations and evaluations in the life insurance industry in this part of the twentieth century?

A. They are.[5]

The court admitted that if the insurance company had known that Donald was living with Nancy, it would not have issued the policy or would have exacted a higher premium, but the court pointed out that it would not have done so only on the basis of Donald's using the word "single." With today's intensive investigation into the private lives of people seeking insurance, it is highly unlikely that you could keep information about your living with someone to yourself. (Whether it is at all relevant or a proper subject of their inquiry is another battle.) So it would be sensible to play it straight. Tell the truth on your application so that you will not be unpleasantly surprised years later when you are about to exercise the policy. The real issues and the ones that should be addressed directly are, Do insurance companies have any right to inquire into the intimate details of our lives? and What is the relevancy of marital status or living situation to whether or not you are a good risk?

Will Your Illegitimate Child Be Entitled to the Proceeds of Your Insurance Policy?

In a life insurance policy, for example, it is customary to designate beneficiaries. If you fail to do so, there is a clause that defines them for you. If this clause says "children," does that mean illegitimate children too? In states that have a strong public policy of restricting the illegitimate child's right of inheritance, such as Georgia and Louisiana, you can expect that "children" does not mean illegitimate children.[6] In those states with a more liberal attitude toward illegitimate children, "children" will include them. A California court reached that conclusion by reasoning that the purpose of life insurance is to provide for maintenance of dependents whom the insured is legally obligated to support; he/she is legally obligated to support illegitimate children; therefore, they must be considered among the intended beneficiaries of life insurance policies.[7]

The reasoning the court in your state chooses will depend on the attitudes it takes toward illegitimate children. It is best to prevent the question of whether "children" means illegitimates from arising by naming the child as the beneficiary of your policy. That is the only way of assuring that he or she will benefit.

Will You Have Any Problem Getting Insurance on Your Life if Your Wife or Husband Has Insurance on Hers or His?

Frank, an aspiring young logic professor, nearly got hit by a truck as he was crossing the street one morning. Concluding that life was a transient thing, he decided to take out a life insurance policy. His wife, Lin, was a medical student at the time and not quite in a financial position to pay for insurance on her life. So Frank thought he would take out two policies, one for himself and one for her. He met with an insurance agent and everything was going along smoothly until Frank brought up the subject of insuring his wife's life. The agent was dumbfounded—"Your wife, what does she need insurance for?" It became clear that the insurance agent believed that only men should be insured; if a man died, his wife would need support; if she died, he could and would continue to support himself. The insurance agent remained convinced that, generically, husbands support wives and that by definition there is no economic loss when a wife dies, despite Frank's efforts to convince him that once Lin started to practice medicine, she would earn more money in a year than he would in five. Frank got the two policies, but the insurance agent went away muttering about the irrationality of logic professors.

The incident reveals an attitude prevalent in the insurance business—women don't need insurance. Unfortunately, this attitude is prevalent among women too, and it is only recently that women are becoming aware that their lives are worth money also. As more women become financially independent, as more women are affected by divorce, as more women enter the labor market, as more men and women realize that housework and child care have economic values, this attitude will change. Once the insurance companies get over their initial surprise, they will be delighted to receive your premiums.

A different kind of problem may arise in an employment context. Many companies limit the amount of life insurance they will issue to a married woman to some proportion of the amount of life insurance her husband has. The articulated theory behind the practice is that a family should not have to pay for "unnecessary" insurance. A more plausible reason may be that it offers an excuse to reduce the employer's contribution to an employee benefit plan. If a company, however, offers different benefits to its female employees than it does to its male employees, it may constitute a violation of the Equal Employment Opportunity Act and is grounds for a complaint.

Can an Employer Deny or Limit Fringe Benefits to an Employee on the Basis that His/Her Spouse Has Coverage?

No. The EEOC guidelines concerning sex discrimination in employment make it unlawful for an employer to discriminate between men and women with regard to fringe benefits.[8] These include medical, hospital, accident, life insurance and retirement benefits, profit-sharing and bonus plans, and leave. Even if an employer says all employees whose spouses have life insurance get 50 percent less coverage than employees whose spouses do not, the policy will be unlawful if it has a discriminatory impact on either sex. In other words, although it is not discriminatory on its face, it may be in effect because more spouses of female employees have, for example, insurance than spouses of male employees. This kind of practice should be brought to the attention of the EEOC.

Can an Employer Offer Benefits to the Wives of Male Employees without Offering Those Benefits to the Husbands of Female Employees?

No. The EEOC guidelines make this an unlawful employment practice. In applying the guidelines, the EEOC has invalidated a group-insurance plan maintained by an employer and union that covered wives of male employees but not husbands of female employees.[9]

Can an Employer Offer Benefits to the Wives of Male Employees without Offering Them to Female Employees?

No. The EEOC guidelines make it an unfair practice. A prevalent example occurs where maternity benefits are available to the wives of male employees but not to the female employees. The EEOC guidelines expressly prohibit that.

Can an Employer Deny Health Benefits to Women Disabled by Pregnancy?

A federal district court has held that if an employer offers a health benefit program (which he is not legally obligated to do), it must cover pregnancy-related disabilities.[10] The issue is now pending before the Supreme Court.[11]

Employers argue that pregnancy should not be covered because it is voluntary and because it costs too much. But it has been held that pregnancy coverage may not be excluded because of cost.[12] It has also been held that pregnancy coverage cannot be excluded as a "voluntary" disability if the plan covers disabilities resulting from such voluntary risks as drinking, smoking, or sports.[13] But neither issue has yet been authoritatively decided.

Can an Employer Deny Pregnancy Benefits to Single Employees?

In all probability, the answer is no. The EEOC guideline that says that an employer may not provide benefits to the wives of male employees if they are not also available to female employees would seem to dictate this response because it does not distinguish between married and unmarried female employees.[14]

In addition, the EEOC prohibits giving benefits to employees of one sex and not the other. Men are entitled to paternity leave just as women are entitled to maternity leave. If a man can get paternity leave whether he's married or not, so should a woman.

The maternity policy of the Leechburg Area

School District required that a female teacher be married in order to be entitled to maternity leave. The policy was challenged as a violation of Section 5(a) of Pennsylvania's Human Relations Act, which prohibits sex discrimination. The school district argued that the purpose of the policy was to ensure the moral qualifications of public school teachers. The Pennsylvania Commonwealth court struck down the policy as discriminatory based on sex. The court said that such a policy, "although facially differentiating only between married and unmarried female teachers, has the effect of creating a condition precedent to the eligibility of an employee for disability leave which must only be met by female teachers, and as such, constitutes sex discrimination under Section 5(a)."[15] In other words, although the policy didn't expressly discriminate on the basis of sex, it had the *effect* of doing so because the policy was not applied to male teachers who fathered illegitimate children.

This is, however, still pretty much an open issue.

Can You Be Denied Employment Fringe Benefits for Living with Someone?

The answer seems to be no—at least no one has brought a complaint about it. Generally, your eligibility for fringe benefits is not dependent on your relationships to or with people; they are not derivative, as are social security benefits. They are usually linked to how much you contribute in premiums or what your employer offers as part of your compensation for employment. Therefore, your marital status or living situation should be irrelevant.

Can You Be Denied a Pension for Living with Someone?

A pension is a form of insurance against retirement: it ensures that when you retire you will receive periodic income. Pensions are financed by the contributions employees and/or employers make over the years they are employed. Like fringe benefits, pension plans have nothing to do with the fact that you are related to or living with someone. What you get out depends on what you put in, so you cannot be denied your pension for living with someone.

Can You Be Denied Credit for Living with Someone?

Credit is a lot like insurance: someone is taking a risk on you. We have seen that insurance companies are very much interested in your private life, especially your marital status and the company you keep. They feel that that knowledge will help them determine what kind of a risk you are. People in the business of granting credit think along the same lines. Their inquiries into your private life are limited by the Fair Credit Reporting Act, as is the case in the insurance business. The information sought must be relevant to the objectives of the inquiry. A correlation between living together and a lack of credit-worthiness has yet to be demonstrated. But it appears to be relevant in the eyes of the credit industry.

Let's say Angela and Michael, who live together, want to buy a house and are seeking a mortgage. It is likely that they will be turned down as poor risks just because they are living together, even if they each hold steady and relatively secure jobs. Does the fact that they are living together have any relevance to their credit-worthiness? None that has been demonstrated.

What should you do if someone refuses you credit and you are living together? The first thing is to find out the contents of the report made on you by the credit-reporting company. Does it state that you are living with someone? Is this the reason you were denied credit? Are there valid reasons—e.g., that you don't have a job? Your next step is to contact a lawyer; depending on the facts, you may sue the lender and/or the credit-reporting agency under the Fair Credit Reporting Act, the antitrust laws, the Constitution, and possibly even the Equal Credit Opportunity Act (ECOA), which prohibits discrimination in the granting of credit on the basis of sex or marital status.[16] If your state has an ECOA, you may seek redress under it as well.

Can a Married Woman Get Credit in Her Own Name and on Her Own Account?

Yes. If a married woman is relying on her own income and assets to establish her credit-worthiness, there is no reason why she cannot obtain credit in her own name, nor is there any reason why she must report her husband's income. Before the ECOA, a married woman faced difficulty in obtaining credit because of state laws denying her capacity to contract and because of the assumption that her income would not be steady.

Now the creditor may ask if she is married only

if the inquiry is to ascertain the creditor's rights. One reason is that in all states the husband is liable for the support of the wife and in some states each is liable for the support of the other. So if a person is married, the creditor can sue his or her spouse for "necessaries" if the spouse to whom credit was granted defaults.

In addition, many states have "family expense statutes" that make both spouses liable for purchases of household items made by either even without the other's permission. If the creditor knows whether the applicant is married, he/she knows whether he/she can sue the other spouse under the family expense statutes in case of default.

A creditor cannot require your spouse to co-sign when you apply for credit except in community property states or if state law requires both signatures.

Can a Creditor Discount a Wife's Income When Extending Credit to Husband and Wife?

Creditors have feared that the wife's income would be merely temporary, subject to pregnancy, and therefore unreliable. They have even asked what methods of contraception a wife used and have tried to get women to sign statements that they would not get pregnant. This is now prohibited by the Equal Credit Opportunity Act.

Before the enactment of the ECOA, a Ms. Hoberman brought suit against Manufacturers Hanover Trust Company because her income was discounted when she and her husband applied for a mortgage.[17]

Manufacturer's settled out of court. They paid $50,000 in money damages, changed their application blanks and policies, and agreed to do three public-service announcements concerning ECOA on prime-time TV. The main problem from now on will be informing people of what their rights are, so that they can assert them if the need arises.

NOTES

1. 15 U.S.C. §§ 1681 et seq., effective April 26, 1971.

2. *Brown* v. *Shield Fire Insurance Company*, Mo. App., 260 S.W.2d 337, 338 (1953).

3. *Hicks* v. *Hatem*, 265 Md. 260, 289 A.2d 325 (1972); *Henderson* v. *State Farm Mutual Auto Insurance Company*, 59 Wis. 2d 451, 208 N.W.2d 423 (1973).

4. *Hunter* v. *Southern Farm Bureau Casualty Insurance Company*, S. Ct. S.C., 129 S.E.2d 59 (1962).

5. *Bunn* v. *Monarch Life Insurance Company*, Ore., 478 P.2d 363 (1971).

6. *Cooper* v. *Melvin*, 223 Ga. 239, 154 S.E.2d 373 (1967).

7. *Turner* v. *Metropolitan Life*, Cal., 133 P.2d 859 (1943).

8. 29 Code of Federal Regulations §§ 1604.9(a)–(b), July 1974.

9. EEOC Dec. No. 71–1100, December 31, 1970.

10. *Gilbert* v. *General Electric*, 375 F. Supp. 367 (E.D. Va. 1974).

11. *General Electric* v. *Gilbert,* 519 F.2d 661 (4th Cir. 1975), appeal to U.S. Supreme Court docketed June 17, 1975, Docket No. 74–1318.

12. 29 Code of Federal Regulations § 1604.9(e) and *Wetzel* v. *Liberty Mutual Insurance Company,* 372 F. Supp. 1146 (W.D. Pa. 1974).

13. *Wetzel* v. *Liberty Mutual Insurance Company,* 511 F.2d 199 (3rd Cir. 1975). On March 23, 1976, the Supreme Court vacated the judgment on a procedural ground, 44 United States Law Week 4350, Docket No. 74–1245.

14. 29 Code of Federal Regulations § 1604.9(d), July 1974.

15. *Leechburg Area School District* v. *Pennsylvania Human Relations Committee,* Pa. Cmnwlth., 339 A.2d 850 (1975).

16. 15 U.S.C. §§ 1691 et seq., effective October 28, 1975.

17. *Hoberman* v. *Manufacturers Hanover Trust Company,* Civil Action No. 73–3279 (S.D.N.Y. 1973).

16 / Consent to Medical Treatment

Let your most morbid fantasies regarding the person you are living with come to mind: Janet being scraped off the sidewalk where she has been hurled from the impact of an out-of-control Jaguar; Steve unconscious on the ski slope after being dragged by his leg, now broken, from the ski lift; Karen moaning with pain; Jim in a coma. Not exactly the kinds of experiences you like to think about, certainly not the kinds of things that you would relish planning for. They are enough to make one wax superstitious —everyone knows that if you make a will you'll die! Similarly, if you so much as think of an accident, it will befall you—or the person with whom you live.

The purpose of talking about these matters— medical emergencies—is not to throw you into a slough of despond, but to point out that this is another area where the law steps in if you are married but leaves you to your own devices—or impotence— if you are not.

Let's continue one scenario. The ambulance comes to a screeching halt; Janet is scooped up by a stretcher. Minutes later she is being wheeled into the emergency room, where they start hooking her up to various wonders of modern technology. Through the din, someone is asking you questions: What's her name? address? age? any allergies? take any drugs?

The doctor turns to you and says, "We're going to have to operate." Janet is unconscious. You start to say, "Well, what are you waiting for?" when you realize it's not your decision to make. What happens? Do they stop preparing for the operation? Do they try to call her family? Do you stand there dry-mouthed, feeling frightened and helpless?

Do You Have the Authority to Consent to Medical Treatment for the Person with Whom You Live? Do You if You Are Married?

First of all, it should be a comfort to know that the medical authorities probably won't let anyone just die. If there is a medical emergency, a doctor and a hospital have the duty to treat the patient. But let's back up a few steps.

Before giving a person medical treatment, a doctor must obtain that person's informed consent, on pain of facing a malpractice suit. A person can only give his/her consent if he/she is capable of doing so—legally or physically. If you are a minor—in most states under eighteen; in some, twenty-one—you cannot legally consent to medical treatment unless you are emancipated. (This basically means that you are financially and otherwise independent of your parents.) If you are not emancipated, the doctor or the hospital has to get one of your parents' consent. Similarly, if you have been adjudged mentally incompetent, someone will have to make these medical decisions for you—either your guardian or a relative. If you are a competent adult, you have legal capacity to consent, but you may lack physical capacity—you may be unconscious.

If there is an emergency in which your life or health is endangered and you cannot give consent, then the hopsital or the doctor is required to treat you anyway. Problems arise in connection with what is the meaning of "emergency." As malpractice suits become more prevalent, members of the medical profession become more reluctant to jump in head first. Where they might have acted more readily years ago, nowadays they are not so eager to ply that scalpel. So even where there is an "emergency," the physician or hopsital will often seek someone's consent.

When the patient is incapable of consent, they seek to obtain the consent of one who can act on the patient's behalf. Traditionally, this means spouse, parent, nonminor child, sibling—next of kin. It does not mean your best friend, or the person who is with you at the hospital, or the person with whom you are living; it means relatives.

If, under the circumstances, you are tempted to pass yourself off as kin, don't. It's too risky. Your friend, the patient, can lose a lot. If something goes wrong and your friend or his/her estate wants to sue the doctor or hospital, the fact that you misrepresented your authority to consent is harmful. It could ruin his/her chances of legal recovery.

If the hospital cannot reach any next of kin (and the problem is not so severe that it qualifies as an emergency), then it may petition the local court to have a guardian declared or to order the treatment to occur.

If you were married, of course, you would have authority to consent.

Is There Any Way You Can Give Each Other Authority to Consent to Medical Treatment?

There appears to be no reason why you cannot make an agreement to that effect. However, this issue has not yet arisen, so you would be breaking new legal ground.

The best approach would be to execute a power of attorney authorizing the person you are living with to consent to operations to be performed on you or to other medical treatment. A power of attorney must be notarized. Put it in your wallet so that if there is an emergency you can produce it. Since hospitals aren't used to that kind of thing, they will probably resist accepting that the power of attorney really does what it says it does. There is no good solution to this problem. The practice will not be accepted until some court gives it the stamp of approval.

Would a Power of Attorney for Medical Treatment Be Upheld against the Wishes of Relatives?

Assuming that your right to consent to medical treatment of yourself is delegable, then your delegation would be good against claims by everyone, including relatives. The theory behind letting your relatives consent for you is that you would wish them to have that power. The law implies that they are your agents. But if you expressly designate someone else as your agent, then there is no longer any need for the implication.

17 / Living Together and Other Countries

What Problems Might You Encounter While Traveling Abroad Together?

To my knowledge, the only places in which people have encountered difficulty are Africa and the Middle East. One married friend whose wife continues to use her own surname reports that they were not permitted to share a berth in a train in Africa. Hotels in France, Italy, and Germany are required by police regulations to have their patrons register on cards that are then sent to the police department. Some say the reason is to monitor and deter prostitution. Others say it is so the police know who's inside the hotel should it be destroyed by fire. Whatever the reason, the regulations have the effect of making it more difficult to keep your private lives private.

The best advice seems to be, when in Rome do as the Romans do. Play it by ear—be sensitive to the values of the country you are visiting. Most areas that invite and rely on tourism as an important source of income will not make things difficult for you. Areas that are not used to foreigners may be less tolerant and more offended by your behavior.

If you are married but have different names, it makes a great deal of sense to bring your marriage certificate or other proof of marriage with you. If any question about your marital status arises, you show your marriage certificate and calmly state that where you come from, a wife does not have to take her husband's name on marriage. That should work. If it does not, adjust. Write a letter to the consulate when you get home.

If you are unmarried, don't broadcast it. Leave your politics at home or be subtle about them, lest you offend the sensibilities of your hosts and make things difficult for yourself.

How Do Other Countries View Living Together by Their Own Citizens?

Some countries tolerate cohabitation more readily than others. While cohabitation occurs to some degree in all nations, it is, as to be expected, most prevalent in countries with a relatively flexible social structure.

Sweden is probably the country with the highest incidence of unmarried cohabitation. In 1974, 6 percent of the adult population of Sweden consisted of unmarried cohabiting persons, an increase from 1 percent in 1968. The increase has been accompanied by a decline in the marriage rate. Whereas in 1966 there were 61,000 marriages, in 1974 there were only 45,000.[1] The Swedish government has not played ostrich, but has chosen to address the situation most candidly. In 1969, the Swedish minister of justice appointed a committee to suggest revisions of the existing family law. As guidelines for the Family Law Reform Committee's work, he stated:

In my opinion a new law ought to be neutral as far as possible in relation to different forms of cohabita-

tion and different ethical beliefs. Marriage has and
should have a central place in family law, but efforts
should be made to ensure that legislation in this
field does not contain any provisions which create
unnecessary difficulties or disadvantages for those
who have children and settle down without getting
married.[2]

His statement reflects an unusual acceptance of living together. It would be viewed as quite radical in
the United States, where twenty states still consider
cohabitation a crime.

The committee's recommendations followed the
sentiment expressed by the Swedish minister of justice. A report by the Swedish Institute, a government
foundation for cultural exchange that publishes information about Sweden, describes the position the
committee took: "The committee argued that certain
legal effects must flow from marriage as distinct from
other forms. But in respect of other kinds of legislation, as in social welfare and taxation, there is fairly
wide consensus that the realities of a family situation
and not its formalities should be the basic starting
point."[3]

The United States is approaching, but is still behind, Sweden in reaching a consensus that the *realities* and not the *formalities* of a family situation
should govern a citizen's legal rights.

What was the result of the committee's efforts?
One major victory was a change in Sweden's rule
denying an unwed father any right to the custody of
his children. The Parliament adopted the new rule
that what is best for the child should prevail. (While
that rule is perhaps implied in the U.S. Supreme
Court decision in *Stanley* v. *Illinois* [see pages 59–
60.], lower courts are years away from implementing

it in the United States.) A second victory was a change in the rule that the person owning the property gets it on separation: Unmarried parties now have equal rights to their common dwelling if they split up, with the dwelling going to the one who needs it most.

The committee also urged reform of the marriage laws in view of the increasing participation of women in the Swedish labor force: in 1967, 54 percent of Swedish women from eighteen to sixty-six; in 1974, 64 percent.[4] Because more women are earning money, they need not be as dependent upon their husbands as they have been. This, the committee thought, should result in a change in the rules governing support during and after the marriage. The Swedish Institute report stated: "The public debate on equality of the sexes has called attention to one disturbing implication of the statutory maintenance liability: in effect, it makes marriage a charitable institution which impedes a desirable development in the direction of a voluntary partnership between two independent individuals who are not bound together by purse strings."[5] In the United States, such a statement would raise cries of horror from some women who say they *like* being dependent.

The committee did not propose to do away completely with support obligations during marriage or alimony afterward. Instead, it was suggested that the practice of awarding permanent alimony only at the end of a long marriage to a wife who had not worked outside the home and had poor chances for self-support should be codified. That has yet to occur, however. While the *practice* in the United States is similar, there is still very little open discussion of making alimony the exception rather than the rule.

And currently, in most states, alimony is available only to women. We are just beginning to ask whether men, too, should be entitled to alimony. There is little comprehension that alimony should be awarded not because one is a woman, but because one is in *need*. Sweden is far closer than the United States to accepting this concept.

I have not come across any nations other than the United States in which cohabitation is a crime. Sanctions against cohabitation in other countries appear to be social and religious, rather than legal.[6] However, the People's Republic of China regards living together and extramarital intercourse rather severely. At one time, they were considered political offenses, prevented presumably by strong peer pressure. It is unclear whether they are still regarded as offenses, but it is clear that living together is just not done in China. The perspective held by the Chinese is described thus:

> The idea that monogamy is the natural way of marriage and that marriage when freed from economic considerations will naturally develop into a unity based on affection is a view held with perfect sincerity by many communists. In this view there is no room for bigamy, adultery and other forms of unlawful intercourse. People who love each other and are of the right age marry each other. If they do not love each other any longer—when the marriage has "collapsed"—they should divorce and marry someone else.
>
> This is made possible by the law and should be practiced in a spirit of earnestness and dignity. . . . it is impossible to love a person whose political views are diametrically opposed and it is a sign of spiritual weakness not to be able to control one's passions: it reflects an immoral and predominantly "feudal" state

of mind. . . . Communist morality is not puritanism for its own sake; it serves the cause of building socialism or communism. Immorality is, therefore, necessarily a political offense, be it "feudal" or "bourgeois."[7]

Sweden and the People's Republic of China exemplify opposite perspectives on cohabitation. Interestingly, the United States view reflects both the puritanism of the Chinese view and the tolerance of the Swedish view.

NOTES

1. Elisabet Sandberg, *Equality Is the Goal: A Swedish Report* (Stockholm: Swedish Institute, 1975), p. 60.
2. Birgitta Alexandersson, *Current Sweden*, No. 8 (Stockholm: Swedish Institute, September 1973). Ms. Alexandersson is a legal adviser to the Swedish Confederation of Trade Unions.
3. *Ibid.*, p. 2.
4. Sandberg, *Equality Is the Goal*, p. 8 n.6.
5. Alexandersson, *Current Sweden*, p. 5 n.7.
6. See Clellan S. Ford, "Sex Offenses: An Anthropological Perspective," *Journal of Contemporary Law and Social Problems* 25 (Spring 1960), p. 227.
7. M. J. Meijer, *Marriage Law and Policy in the Chinese People's Republic* (Hong Kong: Hong Kong University Press, 1971), p. 98.

Postscript

What does all this mean? Is it better, in light of legal considerations alone, to marry or to live together?

Let's summarize the legal pros and cons of living together. On the positive side, if you both work, your taxes will be less than if you were married. A woman won't have trouble keeping her surname, nor will she have trouble establishing her own domicile. She will have full rights to manage and control her own property. Neither of you may be fired under a nepotism rule that prohibits relatives from being employed at the same time. Furthermore, you may have access to a greater child-care deduction than if you were married; and you cannot be held liable for each other's taxes or debts. You do not have to support each other; neither do you have to pay alimony. Probably the greatest legal advantage is that you do not have to go through complex, expensive, and interminable divorce proceedings.

On the negative side, you cannot ensure that your illegitimate child will inherit from the child's father or grandparents if they should die without a will. You have no rights to veterans' benefits, social security, or workmen's compensation derived from the person you are living with. To entitle your illegitimate child to receive these benefits, you must comply with complex state legitimation requirements. If only one of you works outside the home, your income taxes will be higher than they would be if you were married. You cannot take advantage of estate and gift tax breaks for a "child" or "spouse." And you have no rights to each other's property, be it while you are together, after you split up, or if either of you dies.

Then there is a long list of legal negatives of living together that stem from society's disapproval of nonmarital cohabitation. You can be criminally prosecuted for living together in twenty states, with penalties up to $3,000 and three years in prison. You may encounter difficulty obtaining credit, insurance, or housing. You may be fired from your job. You may be denied custody of a child from a former marriage. The constitutionality of these practices is only beginning to be questioned. So living together can make your status very uncertain.

A few conclusions can be drawn. Basically, what's bad about marriage is what's good about living together. Marriage—the legal institution—retains many sexist characteristics: from limitations on a wife's right to contract without her husband's consent to the rules that the husband has the right to choose the wife's domicile and, in some states, that she must take his name. Beyond the remnants of a sexist history, the laws governing marriage reflect a stereotyped view of the functions of husband and wife. The tax laws favor the marital unit in which the wife does the housekeeping and the husband does the money-making. States that allow alimony only to women presume that a woman lacks the ability to provide for herself. In so doing, they perpetuate the belief that men should be the providers. This makes it even more difficult for women to get jobs and thereby become economically independent. Finally, the social security laws presume that the husband supports the wife; in addition, they treat wives who work outside the home the same as wives who are unpaid housekeepers, so that a woman is a worker when she contributes and a wife when she collects.

A man and a woman who are both capable of financial independence and who have the foresight to protect their mutual rights through contracts, wills, and compliance with legitimation procedures, and who do not mind doing some legal battle once in a while to secure their rights to housing, credit, insurance, and employment can live together permanently or temporarily with no difficulty. Most people are not in that position. Few have the awareness or the desire to take a self-protective, preventive approach to their personal relationships. For these people, marriage is probably a good idea ultimately, although living together may well be a perfectly appropriate interim status. For them, marriage defines their rights regarding each other and anticipates contingencies that they will not or cannot foresee, prevent, or provide for. Marriage will not disappear, because it organizes the distribution of societal and private benefits. That is something few people can or have wished to do for themselves.

The issue for the legal profession is twofold. How can we eliminate the barriers to living together that are based on outmoded conceptions of morality? And how can we make marriage egalitarian so that conforming to social goals by marrying no longer means betraying oneself?

What we have been talking about is the process

by which our legal system struggles to mold—but also to reflect—experience.

We are in the midst of social upheaval. The nature of the "family" is being transformed. Our 1950's schoolbook image of the family as Mother, Father, Dick, and Jane is increasingly becoming a fantasy. Now, this may be the family: Father has another set of children living with his first wife and Mother's ex-husband is Jane's biological father; Mother and Father lived together before they got married; and they are thinking of sharing a house with two couples (married, unmarried—who cares?), a few children, three dogs, two cats, and a gerbil.

We see these changes all around us. How can we evaluate them? How can we decide whether they are positive or negative—the signs of societal emancipation or the signs of societal decay?

What will we have lost as our old notions of the family go by the boards? What, if any, were the societal or personal benefits of keeping Ma in the kitchen and Pa in the office? What, if any, were the benefits of strong taboos against premarital sex? Was there a value in making it easy to get into marriage but hard to get out?

Is living together merely a symptom of the hostility so many feel toward others these days? Is it merely an expression of rebellion? Is it the act of people who hate society so much, or who are simply so alienated from it that they wish to ignore its existence and the forms that order it?

Are the people who live togther instead of marrying just plain immature? Do they expect to be able to attain contentment without struggle and compromise? Do they expect to be free without taking responsibility for their acts? For those viewing it that way, living together is an unjustifiable, essentially antisocial act.

However, there are many who find in living together the opportunity to develop a relationship apart from what their conditioning, culture, and the law would dictate for them. It is for these people and in this spirit that this book was written.

Index

ABOUT THE AUTHOR

Nora Lavori is a graduate of Bryn Mawr College and Brooklyn Law School.